# BERNARD MALAMUD

# MODERN LITERATURE MONOGRAPHS

*(continued on last page of book)*

# BERNARD MALAMUD

*Sheldon J. Hershinow*

FREDERICK UNGAR PUBLISHING CO.
NEW YORK

813.09
*H*

# *To Revel and Don*

**Library of Congress Cataloging in Publication Data**

Hershinow, Sheldon J., 1942–
  Bernard Malamud.

  (Modern literature monographs)
  Bibliography: p.
  Includes index.
  1. Malamud, Bernard—Criticism and interpre-
tation.
PS3563.A4Z68     813'.54     79-48077
ISBN 0-8044-2377-6

# Contents

# Chronology

| | |
|---|---|
| 1914 | Bernard Malamud is born in Brooklyn, New York, to Bertha and Max Malamud. |
| 1928-32 | Attends Erasmus Hall High School. |
| 1932-36 | Attends City College of New York; receives bachelor's degree in 1936. |
| 1937-38 | Attends Columbia University. |
| 1940 | Works as clerk in Bureau of Census, Washington, D.C. |
| 1940-48 | Teaches evening classes at Erasmus Hall High School. |
| 1941 | Begins writing short stories. |
| 1942 | Receives master's degree from Columbia University. |
| 1943 | Publishes first stories: "Benefit Performance" in *Threshold* and "The Place Is Different Now" in *American Preface.* |
| 1945 | Marries Ann de Chiara; lives in Greenwich Village. |
| 1947 | A son, Paul, is born. |
| 1948-49 | Teaches evening classes at Harlem Evening High School. |
| 1949-61 | Teaches at Oregon State College, Corvallis, Oregon. |
| 1950 | Stories appear in *Harper's Bazaar*, *Partisan Review*, *Commentary.* |

| | |
|---|---|
| 1952 | *The Natural* is published. A daughter, Janna, is born. |
| 1956-57 | Malamud receives a *Partisan Review* fellowship in fiction; lives in Rome and travels in Europe. |
| 1957 | *The Assistant* is published. |
| 1958 | *The Magic Barrel* is published. Malamud receives the Rosenthal Foundation Award of the National Institute of Arts and Letters for *The Assistant*. |
| 1959 | Receives the National Book Award for *The Magic Barrel*; receives a Ford Foundation Fellowship in humanities and the arts. |
| 1961 | *A New Life* is published. Joins the faculty of Bennington College, Bennington, Vermont. |
| 1963 | *Idiots First* is published. Travels in England and Italy. |
| 1964 | Becomes a member of the National Institute of Arts and Letters. |
| 1965 | Travels in the Soviet Union, France, and Spain. |
| 1966-68 | *The Fixer* is published. Becomes visiting lecturer at Harvard University. |
| 1967 | Wins the National Book Award and the Pulitzer Prize for *The Fixer*. Becomes a member of the American Academy of Arts and Sciences. |
| 1968 | Visits Israel in March. |
| 1969 | *Pictures of Fidelman: An Exhibition* is published. |
| 1971 | *The Tenants* is published. |
| 1973 | *Rembrandt's Hat* is published. |
| 1979 | *Dubin's Lives* is published. |

# 1

# The Writer as Moral Activist

It seems to me that the writer's most important task, no matter what the current theory of man, or his prevailing mood, is
to recapture his image as human being as each of us in his
secret heart knows it to be, and as history and literature have
from the beginning revealed it.

"Address from the Fiction Winner,"
*National Book Award,* 1959[1]

In the quarter-century since the publication of his first
novel, Bernard Malamud has achieved the stature of a
major American author. He has won two National
Book Awards and the Pulitzer Prize for literature.
Reviews of his books abound, and a large body of
criticism testifies to the stimulating effect his writing
has had upon the literary community. One critic
heralded Malamud as a writer who (along with Saul
Bellow) has "brought a new note into the American
novel," one of personal affirmation of the individual in
conflict with impersonal social forces, showing that
"American fiction is still capable of sudden growth,
development and expansion in directions scarcely
predictable."[2] His six novels and four collections of
short stories have gained for Malamud a popular and
critical following unstinting in its praise and respect.

Although the subjects and settings of Malamud's
works vary widely, one characteristic remains consis-
tent throughout: his moral earnestness. In a 1958 interview, Malamud complained that American fiction
"is loaded with sickness, homosexuality, fragmented
man. . . . It should be filled with love and beauty and
hope. We are underselling man."[3] In subsequent inter-

1

views, Malamud has consistently emphasized that he bases all of his writing on a belief in the nobility of the human spirit and that only readers who respect human beings can respect his fiction.

Malamud's commitment to a renewal of faith in humanity is applauded by enthusiastic readers and critics around the world who praise his ability to come close to the center of human feeling. In so "foreign" a place as Japan, at least five of Malamud's books have been translated and are well known among university students and professors. As the novelist Philip Roth said, "What it is to be human, to be humane, is his subject: connection, indebtedness, responsibility, these are his moral concerns."[4]

Although Malamud's stated purpose puts unusual emphasis on the writer's role as a moralist, one ought not forget that his vehicle of expression is fiction. He has emphasized that "artists cannot be ministers. As soon as they attempt it, they destroy their artistry. To me writing must be true; it must have emotional depth; it must be imaginative. It must enflame, destroy, change the reader."[5] In his works, Malamud's moral purpose combines with a complex form of irony that one critic has called "sly" because it often seems to undercut his moral vision at the same time that it affirms it. This infuses Malamud's fiction with an elusive quality that has for a generation both intrigued and frustrated commentators on his work.

A difficulty facing any commentator of Malamud's fiction is that of giving artistic judgments about a moralistic writer. In general, critics devote a great deal of attention to the ideas in Malamud's fiction. However, Malamud is not a probing thinker, and too great an emphasis on his morality and affirmation of human potential can cause one to misjudge his artistic achievement. Yet Malamud deliberately asks to be treated as a moralist; he fully recognizes that good fiction is serious, that it can influence people in profound ways. Thus, critics must separate the moral and aesthetic elements in Malamud's fiction; they have an obligation to comment on its overall effect, as well as to analyze its aesthetic success. In accord with this view, the plan of this monograph is to reserve for a concluding chapter evaluation of Malamud's moral perspective.

Malamud only rarely grants interviews. In a recent session (conducted, according to his wishes, by mail),[6] Malamud stated that he dislikes explaining his work because by describing his intent he may, in a sense, betray it. He fears that people may substitute what he says about his writing for their own imaginative reading of it. He does not like to reveal the sources of his stories, and he emphasizes that thoughtful readers should not confuse the writer's life with his fiction or even devote much effort to relating the two. There is, in fact, a marked contrast between the sobriety of Malamud's private life and the exuberant imagination and zest for life characteristic of his fiction.

Perhaps because of Malamud's desire for privacy, no book-length biography of him has ever been written, and very little information about his life has been included in works of criticism. The following biographical sketch is drawn from a brief entry in the *Current Biography Yearbook* and from scattered biographical information that appears in a handful of interviews.[7]

Bernard Malamud was born in Brooklyn in 1914 to Bertha Fidelman Malamud and Max Malamud. His parents were Jewish immigrants from Russia who eked out a meager living from a small grocery store in the Flatbush section of Brooklyn. Despite their poverty and lack of formal education, they encouraged their son's desire for education and his ambition to become a

writer. His mother, who came from a theatrical family, died at forty-four, when he was only fifteen.
Malamud's experiences in Brooklyn, his close ties with
his parents, and his observation of his neighbors contribute to the rich texture and vitality of many of his
memorable stories and characters.

From 1928 to 1932, Malamud attended Erasmus
Hall High School. He graduated from New York City
College in 1936 and received his master's degree from
Columbia University in 1942. He wanted to teach English in the New York City schools but found teaching
positions scarce in the late days of the Great Depression. Thus, he accepted a federal appointment with
the Bureau of Census in Washington, D.C. While
there, Malamud had short pieces published in the
*Washington Post*.

Returning to New York City and to Erasmus Hall
High School, Malamud taught evening classes to free
his days for writing. He and Ann de Chiara married in
1945 and had a son, Paul, two years later. During this
time his stories were published in *Threshold* and
*American Preface*. In 1948 and 1949 he taught evening
classes at Harlem High School. Stories such as "Black
Is My Favorite Color" and "Angel Levine" express, the
former in a realistic and the latter in a fantastic vein,
Malamud's life in Brooklyn and his involvement in the
lives of blacks, Jews, and other ethnic groups.

In 1949 he accepted a position in the English
Department at Oregon State College, Corvallis, where
he remained until 1961. As a writer teaching without
the customary doctoral degree at a rather tradition-
bound institution, and as an artist at a technical and
agricultural school, Malamud's position was a difficult
one. He taught, for the most part, courses in freshman
composition and an occasional introductory literature
course or short-story class. He earned promotion to

assistant professor in 1954 and to associate professor in 1959.

Malamud is a writer who works well alone—away from centers of literary fads and trends—and so his years at Oregon State were productive ones. In addition to writing stories that appeared in *Harper's Bazaar*, *Partisan Review*, *Discovery*, *Commentary*, *The American Mercury*, *Esquire*, and *The New Yorker*, Malamud published three significant volumes of fiction before leaving Oregon.

His first novel, *The Natural* (1952), brought Malamud to the attention of the literary community as a promising young writer. In 1956, Malamud received the *Partisan Review* fiction fellowship, which enabled him to live in Rome and travel in Europe. The influence of his experiences in Italy can be seen in such stories as "The Maid's Shoes," "The Lady of the Lake," "The Last Mohican," and "Behold the Key." In an interview, Malamud explained that his experience in Italy was greatly enhanced by his wife's Italian background. She had been to Italy and could speak fluent Italian. Through her relatives and acquaintances Malamud quickly became immersed in Italian life.

Malamud's second novel, *The Assistant* (1957), became a critical and popular success almost overnight, and Malamud soon received recognition as a major writer, winning the Rosenthal Award of the National Institute of Arts and Letters and the Daroff Fiction Award of the Jewish Book Council of America. *The Magic Barrel* (1958), Malamud's first collection of short stories, was similarly hailed as the work of a major writer. For *The Magic Barrel*, Malamud won the National Book Award in 1959.

The setting for the next period of Malamud's life was Bennington College in Vermont, where he joined the faculty of the Language and Literature Division in 1961, the year in which *A New Life* was published. This novel, started at the writer's colony of Yaddo, New York, in August 1958, is about a New Yorker who goes West to begin a new spiritual life. It is the story of a Jewish teacher in a non-Jewish milieu, satirically reflecting Malamud's Oregon experiences and the impact of the rural West upon his city-conditioned vision.

In 1963 Malamud's short stories appeared in periodicals as diverse as *Commentary* and *Playboy*. "Naked Nude," one of the Italian stories featuring Arthur Fidelman as protagonist, was awarded *Playboy*'s annual fiction prize. This and some of his other previously published stories were collected in *Idiots First* (1963). In 1964 he became a member of the National Institute of Arts and Letters Book Award Committee.

During the several years after leaving Oregon, Malamud also traveled extensively in France, Spain, and the Soviet Union; the latter became the setting of his fourth novel, *The Fixer* (1966). For *The Fixer*, Malamud received both the National Book Award and the Pulitzer Prize for literature. The following year, Metro-Goldwyn-Mayer made a film version of *The Fixer*, which many reviewers thought lacked the power of Malamud's novel.

Dividing his time, in recent years, between his native New York City and Bennington College, Vermont, Malamud has continued to write finely honed, moving fiction. His four most recent books, while expanding his earlier thematic and artistic concerns, show an increasing diversity of subjects, techniques, and settings that strengthen his standing as a major living American writer.

Malamud's first novel, *The Natural*, is a mythic

treatment of an imaginary baseball hero whose career traces an arc from country bumpkin to the heights of glory and back to obscurity because of a nearly fatal moral weakness. Although it received mixed reviews at the time, a retrospective look shows that many of the early commentators did not fully understand or appreciate *The Natural*'s innovative blending of humor, fantasy, romance, and myth.

With *The Assistant* and *The Magic Barrel*, Malamud developed a distinctive subject and style that allowed a flowering of his extraordinary talent. *The Assistant* goes back to Malamud's Brooklyn childhood for its setting and characters. The protagonist, like Malamud's father, is an impoverished Jewish storekeeper, "a good man" who finds in the spirit of Judaism a soul-saving compassion for humanity. Some of the stories in *The Magic Barrel* (and in *Idiots First*) are set in Italy, but most, like *The Assistant*, return to Brooklyn and the gray lives of impoverished Jewish immigrants.

That many of Malamud's characters are Jews seems fitting. As he explained, "I know them. But more important, I write about them because the Jews are absolutely the very stuff of drama."[8] Out of the rhythms and tonalities of Yiddish-speaking American life in New York City, he creates a fictional world that is at once unique and universal.

Knowing that Malamud is a writer with a powerful moral vision, is of Jewish background, and frequently writes about Jewish characters, one might assume that he is a religious writer—one primarily concerned with a Jewish framework of life. Such a conclusion would miss the mark. Malamud is a secular Jew whose Jewishness is an ethnic identity and moral perspective far more than it is a religious persuasion. What infuse his writing are the aspirations, struggles, and indignities of an ethnic and cultural subgroup—

the Yiddish-speaking Jewish immigrants from eastern Europe. Jewish theology and ritual per se are not the focus. According to Malamud's own testimony, he did not actually learn of Judaism (that is, Jewish religious thought) until he read about it as an adult. In fact, Malamud is sometimes criticized by Jewish publications for failing to include specifically Jewish religious content in his works.

Malamud's Jews struggle in a pitiful existence. Unlike Jews in the works of Sholom Aleichem, Mendele Modher Sforim, and other traditional Yiddish writers with whom he is often compared, Malamud's characters are not practicing Jews, nor are they nourished by a strong sense of community—they suffer in lonely isolation. Yet, they possess instinctive dignity and inbred humanitarianism. They express themselves in a Yiddishized English that may lack elegance but somehow conveys a strong sense of identity. In effect, then, Malamud's characters reflect the experience of East-European Jews as an oppressed people who somehow managed to survive centuries of humiliation and persecution without losing their humanity. Malamud uses Jewishness as an ethical symbol. In his works the Jew becomes a metaphor for the good man striving to withstand the dehumanizing pressures of the modern world. His characters hold their ethical stances out of a sense of humanity, and this humanity is only indirectly linked to their religious heritage.

By 1958, then, the subject of Malamud's most characteristic fiction had become clear: Jews, representative of mankind, living in poverty and undergoing existential anguish. Most often they were portrayed via a unique fusion of ground-gripping realism and high-flying fantasy, all seasoned by a tough, biting comic irony of the kind often associated with Jewish comedians such as Mort Sahl, Lenny Bruce, or Woody Allen.

*The Fixer* differs from Malamud's previous novels in several ways. It is his only work based upon an actual historical incident, the Mendel Beiliss case, an infamous example of cruelty and injustice revealed in the degrading persecution of a Jewish handyman. And unlike Malamud's other novels, the setting is tsarist Russia rather than America. Most of the themes that Malamud had introduced into his earlier works are here refined and reworked into a powerful, controlled, and effective statement of human possibilities and limitations.

*Pictures of Fidelman: An Exhibition* is a compilation of all the stories about Arthur Fidelman, a failed American painter in Italy. It develops a concern apparent in some of Malamud's earliest stories: the tension between life and art. The most broadly comic of Malamud's works, *Pictures of Fidelman* is also the most experimental. Malamud has explained that he had conceived the idea for the collection soon after writing "The Last Mohican" in Rome in 1957. At that time he had worked out an outline of other Fidelman stories, planning to have the adventures develop one theme in the form of a picaresque novel. The collection does, in fact, have a development of character and theme close to that of a novel.

The stories in *Pictures of Fidelman* drew critical attention to another aspect of Malamud's art: his brilliant adaptation of Yiddish folk materials. Many critics recognized in the protagonist, Arthur Fidelman, a contemporary version of the traditional Yiddish folk figure, the schlemiel—a comic bumbler whose bad luck is exceeded only by the goodness of his heart. After publication of these stories, critics increasingly began to comment on Malamud's use of the

schlemiel and other Jewish folk characters in his
earlier works, especially in *The Assistant, The Magic
Barrel, The Fixer,* and *Idiots First.* Malamud's use of
Yiddish folklore has brought him the label of "Jewish
writer," a classification he rejects.

*The Tenants* draws upon Malamud's earlier experience as a teacher in Harlem and his lifelong concern with ethnic groups, especially Jews and blacks. In
an empty and crumbling tenement of the inner city,
two men—a black and a Jew, both writers—meet, and
their confrontation as rivals becomes a paradigm for
human relations in our time. Here Malamud once
again writes of the sordid wasteland of back alleys in a
modern city, but he incorporates more elements of
fantasy than appeared in any of his novels since *The
Natural.* The symbolic confrontation of Jew and black
takes place in a surrealistic atmosphere that blends
realism and fantasy so thoroughly that the reader cannot always determine with certainty where reality
ends and dream begins. In *The Tenants,* Malamud
fulfills another of his stated artistic goals: to recreate in
his fiction the sense of uncertainty that is part of life.
For Malamud, ambiguity and surprise play a vital role
in both the drama of life and the richness of art.

His fourth collection of short stories, *Rembrandt's
Hat* (1973), reflects Malamud's fascination with the
tension between life and art, now transferred from
Italy to Malamud's native New York. These stories
confirm what some critics have long claimed: that
Malamud is a master storyteller, one of the finest
writers of our day, in the genre of the short story as
well as the novel.

*Dubin's Lives* (1979) is a long and ambitious novel
about love, marriage, and aging. It has received very
mixed reviews. This novel reveals a surprising new side
of Malamud. Centering on a middle-aged biographer,
a transplanted New Yorker, who struggles to grow old

gracefully, the story takes place in rural upstate New York. Drawing on twenty-years of rural living, first in Oregon and then in Vermont, Malamud sensitively evokes the beauty of the New England landscape. Usually associated with blighted cityscapes, Malamud here demonstrates his continuing ability to expand the range of his art.

✳ Despite the diversity of techniques, subjects, and settings in his fiction, Malamud creates a unified moral vision based upon the values of humanism, which have been central to Western civilization since the ancient Greeks. As a writer, Malamud starts by assuming certain shared values—the primacy of human aspiration, the power of love, the transcendent potential of meaningful suffering and self-sacrifice, the beauty of the human spirit. This humanistic vision, perhaps because of Malamud's early family life among Jewish immigrants, was especially influenced by the central literary and religious book of the Judeo-Christian tradition, The Old Testament, particularly the "Book of Job."

Despite his extensive use of Jewish characters and settings, Malamud is very much an American writer who works within an American literary tradition. Many critics agree that American literature has been heavily influenced by the romance. Hawthorne, for example, was convinced that romance (or the romance-novel) was the predestined form of American fiction. In his introduction to *The Scarlet Letter* he says that the problem confronting the American author is to find "a neutral territory, somewhere between the real world and fairyland, where the Actual and the Imaginary may meet, and each imbue itself with the nature of the other." In other words, Hawthorne conceived of the field of action as a state of mind rather than a place—the borderland of the

human mind where the actual and the imaginary in-
termingle. The only absolute requirement of romance,
Hawthorne adds in his preface to *The House of the
Seven Gables*, is that it must not "swerve aside from
the truth of the human heart." Henry James echoed
this view when he defined the essence of romance as
"disconnected and uncontrolled experience—uncontrolled by our general sense of 'the ways things happen.' . . ."9 From *The Scarlet Letter* and *Billy Budd*
down through *The Red Badge of Courage* to *Light in
August* and *The Old Man and the Sea*, American
literature has demonstrated a moralistic and
allegorical thrust. The value system carried within this
tradition has usually been broadly humanistic rather
than narrowly religious, emphasizing such concerns as
the liberation of the individual human spirit and the
need for love, faith, and respect in human relationships. Malamud has emphasized that his sources are
Hawthorne, James, Twain, and Hemingway more
than Sholom Aleichem and I. L. Peretz.10 Following
the lead of Hawthorne, Malamud writes moral
allegories intended to delight readers while teaching
them lessons of faith and humane behavior.

Another influence on Malamud's writing comes
from the philosophy of existentialism, which
originated in Europe and which emphasizes the existence of a meaningless social disorder, referred to in
existential writings as absurdity. To many traditional
humanists, existentialism at first appeared to be a rejection of the humanist tradition because it seemed to
deny an inherent meaning in life, but the perspective
of time has shown it to operate largely within the
framework of humanistic values.11 Although existentialism posits the idea that man is alone in a godless
world that has no inherent meaning, one effect of this
tenet has been to put greater emphasis on man's individual potential. Suffering anguish and despair in

his loneliness—a universal condition—man may, nevertheless, become what he wishes by the exercise of free will.

For the existentialists neither a universal system of moral order nor the influence of society and social custom can provide meaning for an individual's life; each person must find meaning for himself. This cannot be accomplished through reason alone—love, compassion, and moral commitment are also necessary. Morality, according to existentialists, has validity only when it results from the individual's active participation in the difficult process of forging personal meaning out of universal chaos. As a writer influenced by existentialism,[12] Malamud demonstrates an implicit respect for self. His protagonists characteristically transcend the disorder that surrounds them, finding meaning in the power of love and moral commitment.

Artistically, Malamud seasons his humanistic values with a deft use of irony. There are many kinds of irony, but in its simplest sense, irony results when the implied attitudes toward what is said are in contrast to those literally expressed. By extension, any action or observation that draws attention to a sharp and unexpected contrast between reality and our expectations or beliefs is said to be ironic. As a technique for creating tragic effects and for making moral judgments, irony has a long history stretching back to the Greeks. In the nineteenth century, irony became more than a characteristic technique for transmitting attitudes and judgments—for many writers it came to embody a way of looking at the world, the natural corollary to a vision of human weakness in conflict with a universal morality. For existential writers irony takes on a more chameleonlike appearance; it implies that the writer does not unreservedly commit himself to any one attitude or outlook; he always includes an ironic awareness of opposite and complementary attitudes. For example, an irony of ambivalence is virtually built into Sartre's view of man as a creature "condemned" to be free.

In the hands of a skillful writer like Malamud, the ironic stance can be used to create subtle effects ranging from comic deflation to bitter denunciation, but characteristically his irony underscores the complexity and ambiguity of life. Malamud uses the ironic perspective as a means of conveying the uncertainty and ambiguity—the existential anguish—of life; he also casts irony within an unmistakably humanistic framework, projecting a sharp contrast between situations that are brutal, uncivilized, and dehumanizing and ideals that are noble, sane, and humane.

Malamud frequently uses a very special sort of double-edged comic irony. From writers in the Yiddish folk tradition of eastern Europe Malamud adapted the most singular and distinctive ingredient in his literary recipe: a tough Jewish humor (sometimes called Jewish irony). Jewish humor does not stem from the religion of the Jews—the Old Testament and the Talmud are singularly humorless works. Jewish humor derives instead from the social situation of East-European Jews as a minority precariously surviving within the larger Christian culture. A proud people, these Jews were acutely aware of their lowly status. They were the Chosen People of God but also the oppressed people of the Polish or Russian village. Humor came to be used as a way of bridging the gap between their spiritual aspirations and their actual material situation. As faith in Judaism weakened and skepticism increased, the contrast between the hope and the reality became more and more ironic. This unwanted marriage of circumstance and belief gave birth to the folk figure of the schlemiel, the good-hearted but ineffectual comic bumbler who habitually stumbles into misfortune. The sleight of hand in his comic actions is intended to persuade us that his weakness is really a kind of strength.

A traditional story has it, for example, that a Russian captain, before an important battle, instructed each of his men to choose one of the enemy to engage in battle. The Jewish soldier asked if the captain would please point out his man right away so that he could "maybe come to an agreement with him." As outrageous, and even absurd, as this schlemiel's innocence may seem, his suggestion makes sense within a humanistic framework; he is nonmilitary, not antimilitary. In this way, the impulse of the joke and of schlemiel literature in general, is deliberately to call in question the political and philosophical status quo.

Malamud adapted such Yiddish folk materials for his own artistic ends, using Jewish humor as a means of unifying his literary creations. As an ironic technique, Jewish humor provides a sort of double vision, capable of sustaining hope while recognizing despair. As an artistic brush stroke, it provides a consistency of tone and mood that incorporates both the tragic and the comic. As a moral perspective, Jewish humor combines the values of humanism with the gritty reality of an everyday life that seems existentially absurd. Malamud's use of Jewish humor provides the key to understanding both his attitude toward human existence and his technique as a writer.

# 2

•••••••••••••••••••••••••••••••••••••••••••••••••••••••

# The Hero in the Modern World: *The Natural*

Malamud's first novel, *The Natural*, differs markedly from his later works. It is sometimes described as a baseball story, but actually baseball is only the background from which Malamud draws his real subject: the plight of the mythic hero in the modern world. Unlike the traditional boys books, Malamud's novel embodies an intellectual's view of baseball as a symbolic representation of American values. And unlike Ring Lardner, who used baseball as a way to show the seamy side of American life, Malamud uses a heroic style, full of romantic exaggeration, whimsical inventiveness, and magical fantasy. As Leslie Fiedler has pointed out, the baseball player is "the last symbol . . . of the heroic."[1] He is the perfect embodiment of the American Dream—a hero whose success depends solely upon his talent and perseverence. The game itself is a symbolic reenactment of the rags-to-riches theme so much a part of the fiber of American democracy.

In a recent interview, Malamud revealed that before starting work on *The Natural* he had no interest in or knowledge of baseball, but in preparation for his novel, he read about what was, in 1952, still unquestionably "the national pastime." Out of baseball ritual and lore Malamud distilled the heroic component of the game as a measure of man, similar in nature to Homeric battles, chivalric tournaments, or the Arthurian quest for the Holy Grail. The shooting of Eddie Waitkus in 1949 by an emotionally disturbed girl in her Chicago hotel room; Pete Reiser's fatal crash against the outfield wall; Chuck Hostetler's fall between third and home base when he could have won the sixth game of the 1945 World Series; Wilbert Robinson's attempt to catch a grapefruit dropped from an airplane, Rabbit Maranville's penchant for crawling on window ledges; Babe Ruth's hitting a home run for a dying boy—these and other legendary episodes from baseball history all appear in *The Natural.*

The novel is divided into two parts. A short section titled "Pre-Game," which serves as a kind of prologue for the novel, follows the adventures of nineteen-year-old pitcher Roy Hobbs as he journeys by train to Chicago for a tryout with the Cubs. He is accompanied by Sam Simpson, an alcoholic former major-league catcher and scout who hopes to use his discovery of Roy to resurrect his scouting career. Off the field Roy is a naive, self-centered country bumpkin; apparently on a train for the first time, he worries how much to tip the porter, who humors him with mock understanding, as if speaking to a child. However, with his homemade bat, Wonderboy, fashioned from a tree that had been split by lightning and seeming to possess an energy all its own, Roy is a superbly gifted ballplayer ready to become "the best there is."

Also on the train is Walter (the Whammer) Wambold, aging American League batting champion and three-time winner of the Most-Valuable-Player award. When the train is mysteriously delayed, Roy and the others wander over to a nearby carnival, where the Whammer displays his prowess at a batting cage and Roy attracts a crowd by throwing baseballs at milk bottles. As the rivalry builds to its inevitable confrontation, Sam bets that Roy can strike out the Whammer with three pitches. After the third pitch, the Whammer drops the bat and returns to the train, "an old man."

Roy's triumph brings him to the attention of Harriet Bird, a girl with "heartbreaking legs," who guards a shiny black hatbox as jealously as Roy guards Wonderboy. Excited by Roy's victory in "the Tourney," she tells him he is like "David jawboning the Goliath-Whammer, or was it Sir Percy lancing Sir Maldemer, or the first son (with a rock in his paw) ranged against the primitive papa?" Roy's spirit soars, and he tells Harriet, "I'll be the best there ever was in the game."

"Is that all?" Harriet asks. Unable to understand how there could be anything more to life than baseball, Roy flounders. Harriet turns out to be the mysterious woman Roy had heard about who shoots promising young athletes with silver bullets. Soon after, in a scene in a Chicago hotel room, Roy, Wonderboy in hand, reaffirms his determination to become the best player who ever lived. Like a priestess who enacts a magical rite, Harriet reaches into her mysterious hatbox, draws out a gun, and shoots Roy in the stomach with a silver bullet as Roy tries vainly to catch the bullet with his bare hand.

The main narrative of the novel, in the section entitled "Batter Up," takes place fifteen years later. Roy is ashamed of his nearly fatal "accident" in Chicago, but he is determined to begin a new life after years of wandering and working at odd jobs. Coarser, if no wiser, Roy (now, like Babe Ruth, an outfielder rather than a pitcher), tries out with the New York Knights, a team that has amassed a record number of losses. In order to win a starting spot in the lineup, Roy must displace the Knights' current left fielder, batting champion Bump Bailey, a gorillalike practical joker, who looks out solely for himself and whose batting

prowess (he is the league's best hitter) does little to inspire his teammates. The rivalry ends when Bump,
trying valiantly to match Roy's flawless fielding,
crashes into the left-field wall and dies of his injuries.
With the aid of Roy's superhuman feats, the team now
begins a miraculous drive for the elusive pennant.

Roy's new spiritual father is Pop Fisher, the aged
manager of the Knights and a former major-league
player himself, who hopes to lead the Knights to the
world championship. Wise in baseball strategy and
concerned only with the team's performance and
welfare, Pop Fisher enlists Roy's aid—and Roy vows to
help him. Pop's ambition, however, is being thwarted
by the forces of evil in the form of Judge Banner, a
profit seeker who owns sixty percent of the Knights'
stock. Pop had sold stock to the Judge with the stipula-
tion that the manager would retain control over player
deals "as long as he lives." Yet he is slowly losing control. The Judge, who lives in a tower overlooking the
field, is able to harrass the manager in an effort to
force Pop to resign, so that the Judge can seek profits
rather than victory. The Judge is not alone in his cor-
rupt attempt to dominate the game. The power behind him is Gus, the supreme bookie, a modern-day
Merlin the Magician, who uses the magic of statistics
and knows that playing the percentages pays off in the
long run.

At the very moment of success, the team's drive
for the pennant is thwarted by Roy's fatal attraction to
Memo Paris. The niece of Pop Fisher and former
girlfriend of Bump Bailey, Memo has gone into
mourning for Bump, declaring to Roy, with comic exaggeration, that she belongs strictly to a dead man.
The more Memo rebuffs Roy, the more he desires her.
Pop warns that she will "weaken your strength," but
even when Roy discovers that she is in league with Gus

and the Judge, his hunger continues unabated.

Roy's unsatisfied lust for Memo shifts to a more infantile, and equally insatiable, hunger for food; he begins gobbling down larger and larger portions with "a feeling of both having something and wanting it the same minute he was having it." Using Roy's monumental appetite as a way of fulfilling her secret desire to revenge Bump's death, Memo (using Gus's money) prepares a gargantuan feast for Roy and the team the night before a crucial game. As he approaches the seductive Memo in her hotel room, a bellyache hits like "a bolt of shuddering lightning" in the "shattered gut." As he is losing consciousness, Roy dreams of Memo as a "singing green-eyed siren" and then imagines himself being sucked down in a whirlpool of dirty toilet water.

Awakening in a nearby maternity hospital, Roy is told by a doctor that he will recover in time to play in the final game of the season on whose outcome the elusive pennant rests—but the game will be his last. Because of high blood pressure, he must give up baseball forever. Memo now reveals herself as the bitch-goddess of the American Dream who demands a husband who can provide her with expensive things: a house of her own, a maid to clean it, a car, a fur coat. And so it is that Roy accepts a payoff from the Judge to throw the crucial playoff game. Near the end of the game, however, Roy decides that he can not go through with the fix. With sudden determination he swings with all his rediscovered might, but Wonder-boy splits in half with a thunderous roar and a blinding flash of light, leaving Roy symbolically impotent. With one last time at bat, Roy faces young Herman Youngberry, fresh off the farm. Seeing around the young pitcher "a fog . . . full of ghosts and snowy scenes," Roy "struck out with a roar," walking away from the plate, like the Whammer before him, an old man.

In a final scene Roy repudiates the betrayal by climbing the shadowy steps of the tower to throw the bribe money at the Judge. On the street outside, Roy, like Shoeless Joe Jackson of the 1919 Chicago Black Sox, must listen as a newsboy, carrying a stack of papers spreading word of the suspected sellout to the world, implores hopefully, "Say it ain't true, Roy."

As many critics have pointed out, *The Natural* involves the seemingly unlikely combination of the myths of the Grail Knight and the Fisher King—that is, the kinds of myths embedded in medieval romances about King Arthur and the Knights of the Round Table[2]—with the contemporary national mystique of professional baseball. By melding the Arthurian quest with a baseball story, Malamud expands the quest beyond time, making Roy Hobbs's baseball career symbolic of the human psychological and moral situation. Malamud's tale is mythic in the sense that it provides a symbolic ordering of experience, expresses and codifies certain beliefs, contains models of moral behavior, and embodies a view of the world. Thus, in *The Natural* Malamud aligns himself with the ancient literary tradition of the romance, the roots of which extend far back into the Middle Ages. As Richard Chase and others have pointed out, romance is characterized by freedom from the demands of realistic portrayal, by a tendency to plunge into the underside of consciousness, by an inclination to veer toward the mythic, symbolic, and allegorical.[3]

Expressing the extreme contradictions that shaped the American imagination, romance found a home in the works of some of our greatest nineteenth-century writers—Cooper, Thoreau, Hawthorne, Melville. By the turn of the twentieth century, however, romance had seemingly succumbed to the growing impulse of realism, which endeavored to evoke reality through the accumulation of accurate, verifiable detail. Reaching its peak in the 1920s and 1930s, realism was (and is) generally considered to be the most important mode of American fiction. However, elements of romance have continually infiltrated and modified the predominant practices of realism, even bursting forth into clear view from time to time, as in the works of William Faulkner. The post–World War II period has seen a resurgence of romance elements in American fiction. *The Natural* is one of the first novels after World War II in which the myths and techniques of medieval romance have been deliberately and openly adapted to suit the purposes of a modern writer.

The opening section establishes the mythic pattern of the novel: a young hero sets out in search of fame and fortune, encounters and conquers an ageing hero, only to be laid low by a mysterious temptress. It is the stuff of ancient fertility myths—myths of dying and reviving gods, of youthful heroes replacing the aged, of the son replacing the father—embodying the seasonal cycle of change and here transformed by Malamud into a peculiarly American form. The main body of the novel repeats the mythic pattern of a psychic wound inflicted by a seductive temptress as the hero again fails to achieve his quest. Malamud adds reminders of the symbolism of Arthurian legend: a team called the Knights engages in a quest for the elusive pennant (the Holy Grail) under the guidance of Pop Fisher (the Fisher King).

In developing his mythic theme, Malamud maintains a tone that is comic and surrealistic, as wild flights of fantasy raise baseball superstition to the level of myth. Roy's first hit, for example, knocks the cover off the ball, magically ending a drought (bringing three days of continuous rain) and reversing the fortunes of the Knights. Wonderboy flashes in the sun, blinding Roy's opponents. The charismatic hero brings to his previously demoralized teammates the regenerative force of a god.

As the Knights make their drive for the pennant, the world of the novel remains fluid and magical. Characters from the first part of the novel reappear in slightly different forms, giving Roy the opportunity either to overcome or to reenact the failure of the past. The Whammer reappears as Bump Bailey, the league's current leading hitter. Sam Simpson is metamorphosed into Roy's new spiritual father, the Knights' manager Pop Fisher. The first siren, Harriet, is replaced by Memo Paris, the vindictive temptress who leads Roy to his final ruin.

Clearly, the game of baseball becomes a metaphor for life. It represents the moral world Roy enters when he joins the Knights. It is the oversimplified, black-and-white world characteristic of medieval romance. The powers of evil (the Judge and Gus, representing greed, corruption, death) oppose the forces of good (Pop Fisher, representing idealism, humanity, life), with the dark forces slowly but inevitably gaining sway. Yet Roy possesses the supernatural generative power of such mythic heroes as Achilles and Sir Percival. His efforts can tip the balance. And they do, at least for a while. However, Roy has no comprehension of his role in the moral battle; he does not even recognize that such a cosmic struggle exists. He can think only of himself—his own glory, his own ambitions, his own physical desires. This lack of moral awareness is what causes his dramatic double failure—first in the prologue and again in the main portion of the novel.

The moral weakness caused by Roy's egoism is underscored after Roy indirectly causes the death of Bump Bailey and replaces him in the starting lineup. Most of the fans and sportswriters see no difference between the two players. One newspaper goes so far as to print pictures showing "the living and the dead facing each other with bats held high," demonstrating how alike they were physically. Roy's likeness to Bump is underscored when, in the depths of a slump, Roy imagines he sees the ghost of Bump in his hotel room. Then he slowly realizes it is his own face staring at him from a mirror. In this way Malamud makes clear that for Roy to become a genuine American mythic hero he must live up to the ideals of honesty and fair play that his role as baseball hero requires of him. If he does not attain the spiritual stature to complement his physical attributes, he will become a mock hero, a Bump Bailey, rather than a Fisher King.

Roy's character flaw is counteracted by the influence of Iris Lemon, a woman in Chicago who brings Roy out of his slump by rising up in the stands as an expression of support, metaphorically spreading an "unbelievable fragrance" in the air, and helping Roy renew his confidence in himself. After the game Roy meets the girl and they drive to a secluded spot on Lake Michigan. Roy is slowly won over by the life-giving power of this modern-day Lady of the Lake and he tells her the closely guarded secret of his past—the sordid shooting in a Chicago hotel room.

It is Iris who introduces the central theme of *The Natural.* Her words reveal the reasons for Roy's failures: people must learn through their suffering. "We have two lives, Roy, the life we learn with and the life we live with after that. Suffering is what brings us toward happiness." But Roy is unable to understand the lesson. "I am sick of all I have suffered."

At the end of the novel it is Iris's presence in the stands that causes Roy, belatedly, to renounce the fix. The final scene suggests that Roy is finished as a baseball player but not as a man. Seeing Memo for the first time as the vindictive temptress she is, Roy begins to understand the failures of his life. As he leaves the Judge's domain, he fights an overwhelming self-hatred. Roy finally realizes that because he has refused to learn from the sufferings of the past, he must now face more. We know that Roy will not repeat the same mistakes again, for he can now understand Iris's wistful question, "When will you grow up, Roy?" Malamud implies that only when Roy loses his self-centeredness is he in a position to gain his new and natural life with Iris and their child she carries. Roy must be able to learn from his suffering before he can realize that if he tries to ignore his past he will be destined to relive it. The affirmation is muted but clear. As in all of Malamud's fiction, success can only be gained at the price of failure; the hero can only gain moral redemption at the price of psychic suffering.

Such, then, are the plot, symbols, myths, and themes—the stuff of which *The Natural* is composed—yet a discussion of these basic elements paints a curiously incomplete picture, for it is the style that provides a delightful comic vitality capable of uniting the disparate elements of the narrative. For example, Malamud skillfully uses dream sequences to create a sense of wondrous nonreality. Sometimes the dreams reveal insights into character, sometimes they contribute to thematic concerns, and other times they raise baseball lore to the level of myth. From Sam's fitful dream about discovering a whole team of slugging rustic giants to Roy's vision of Iris as a golden-haired mermaid, the dream sequences all blur the lines between reality and fantasy, lending the novel the silvery aura of a moonlit dreamscape. Sometimes Roy himself cannot tell the difference between dream and reality, as when he becomes convinced that he and Memo have run down a boy he has seen in his dreams. (Memo says the thud they heard must have been caused by a log in the road).

The diction combines lyrical flights of poetic fancy, the gloomy language of psychic suffering, and the snappy slang of baseball to create a delightful comic juxtaposition that actualizes, as one commentator has pointed out, the basic tension of the book between transcendent myth and earthy reality, a yoking of the epic and the mundane.[4] The duel between Roy and the Whammer, for example, is described with all the grandeur of an epic battle. The Whammer "loomed up gigantic," his bat held like "a caveman's ax." He waited "a long light-year . . . for [the] globe to whirl into the orbit of his swing so he could bust it to smithereens that would settle with dust and dead leaves into some distant cosmos." But when the pitch arrives, the Whammer twists around like a top while the ball "hit with a whup into the cave of Sam's glove." Sometimes the contrasting elements appear in alternating passages or sentences. At other times the juxtaposition occurs within a single sentence. The result is a sort of rhythmic union of myth and actuality ripe with both the grandeur of epic possibilities and the disappointment of worldly defeats.

Unfortunately, Malamud is unable to maintain the balance. The tone of the novel wavers between the comic fantasy of mythic exaggeration and the moral seriousness of Malamud's concern with suffering. The novel has other weaknesses, as well. Because Malamud was not a fan and learned about baseball only by reading the lore, he was freed from the constraints of realism, but his lack of first-hand knowledge causes a certain ineptness in his handling of the details of the game. A more serious flaw is that his symbolic use of the machinery of the Arthurian legends often seems clever but superfluous, and even distracting. Throughout the novel Malamud is unable to resist the temptation to include clever comic scenes that sometimes stretch credibility beyond the breaking point. For example, Roy first meets Gus, the bookie, in a symbolic visit to the underworld, when he is taken to the Pot of Fire nightclub, where half-naked chorus girls are chased by devils with pitchforks. Here Roy loses bet after bet with high stakes on seemingly chance occurrences as Gus demonstrates his mastery of fate. But Roy creates some magic of his own. Grabbing the bookie's nose, Roy produces a stream of silver dollars and follows that with a salami, a dead herring, and other wondrous objects. As Gus turns red with embarrassment, Roy presses his advantage, grabbing Gus's "beak" and twisting it until it sheds more silver dollars. Only later does the reader learn that Roy had secretly borrowed a magic act from backstage. The scene succeeds in capturing a sense of magical enchantment, but the reader can not help feeling that he has been tricked by Malamud's magic just as Gus has been made to look a fool by Roy's sleight of hand.

This criticism may seem to give unnecessary attention to an episode that is like a comic-strip box in asking not to be taken literally, but the point is that Malamud possesses a creative power with words that time and again lifts the reader into the wondrous realm of the mythic imagination while at the same time forcing him to remain aware of mundane realities. The balance is a delicate one that is destroyed whenever Malamud shows more intellectual cleverness than artistic judgment. *The Natural* suffers from a lack of control, but it provided literary lessons that the author learned well.

In spite of its weaknesses, *The Natural* is an impressive first novel, a book enjoyed by a wide variety of readers who have no special knowledge of baseball or Arthurian legends but who can respond to the fluid and magical world of the romantic imagination.

# 3

•••••••••••••••••••••••••••••••••••••••••••••••••••••••

# The Prodigal Son Returns:
## *The Assistant*

*The Assistant* was an immediate success, attaining in only a few years the status of an American classic. It also elevated Malamud to the status of a major living American writer; it is the literary cornerstone upon which his reputation continues to rest.

The first part of the novel ushers in the daily hardships of Morris Bober, immigrant owner of a small Brooklyn grocery store, who is slowly being driven out of business by a fancy delicatessen-grocery recently opened around the corner. In the opening chapter, Malamud describes the unremitting burden of Morris's daily life in the style of literary naturalism. Rising at six in the morning to sell a three-cent roll to a "sour-faced, gray haired Poili sheh," Morris begins his daily routine of drudgery and frustration. Although set in mid-twentieth-century America—a time of prosperity—the story conveys an overpowering feeling of Depression hardship. Logging long, empty hours in a store devoid of comfort, Morris manages to eke out a living for himself, his wife, Ida, and his daughter, Helen, only by remaining open until eleven at night. Every afternoon he escapes the gloom of the store by retreating to his upstairs apartment for a nap, his "one refreshment."

Two holdup men appear one night near closing time. Unwilling to believe the $13 in Morris's cash drawer can be his entire take for the day, one of the men pistol-whips him. Sick of his meager existence and filled with self-disgust, Morris bitterly denounces the years of failure and the false hope of success in America.

Into this setting comes a young drifter, an outsider, Frank Alpine. He begins to hang around the store, helping Morris in small ways and asking to be taken on as an assistant in order to gain experience. Morris insists that the store cannot support an employee and sends him away. When he stumbles across Frank asleep in the cellar and learns that he has lived for a week on a daily bottle of milk and two rolls stolen from his doorstep each morning, Morris relents. Ida is outraged at having a goy (non-Jew) in her house, but when Morris's head wound reopens, Frank takes it upon himself to run the store while Morris recovers. He has a way with customers and improves business; the Bobers reluctantly allow him to stay on—"A goy brings in goys," Morris says.

Ida Bober views Frank with suspicion as the "goyish" enemy within, who can be up to no good; above all she is fearful that he will try to seduce her daughter. Indeed, he does make such advances. From the beginning, however, Helen senses something evasive and hidden in Frank. Slowly, she overcomes her distrust of him, and he resolves to become the sensitive person she wants him to be. Nonetheless, he continues to devise schemes for luring her into his room.

One day Morris catches Frank stealing money from the cash drawer and tells him to leave. During Frank's ensuing exile, the Bobers suffer almost as much as he does. Morris and Ida become frenzied at the rapid decline of business, having discovered that the previous increase in trade was due not so much to their sociable assistant as to the illness of the grocer around the corner. The delicatessen closes, but a new, larger self-service store opens that will surely drive Morris into bankruptcy. At this point, Morris accidently leaves the gas to his bedroom heater turned on and is taken to the hospital. Frank returns and again takes over the store, explaining that he owes something to Morris.

In order to keep the business afloat, Frank finally takes a job at an all-night coffee shop, working from ten at night to six in the morning. When Morris returns, Frank confesses what the reader has already realized, that he was one of the men who robbed Morris. Morris surprisingly replies, "This I already know, you don't tell me anything new." But Morris cannot forgive Frank for his pilfering after being taken into the store and sends him away once again. Not long after, Morris dies of pneumonia, and Frank takes over the store again, this time for good.

In a final brief chapter, Frank continues to support the family, getting back each morning from his nocturnal labors in time to sell the "Poili sheh" her roll. He so resembles Morris now that even the salesmen use Yiddishisms freely with him. Wanting to give Helen a gift of love, he offers to finance her college education; she accepts. Helen realizes that "because of something in himself—something she couldn't define," Frank has "changed into somebody else." When she thanks him for running the store and supporting the family, he is able to say truthfully, not what he said earlier, "I owe something to Morris," but rather, "It's just my way." The new life has become permanent.

The novel ends with the brief explanation that one day in April Frank had himself circumcised and felt both "enraged and inspired" by the pain between his legs. "After Passover he became a Jew."

Central to the novel's theme and impact is the characterization of Morris Bober. He is a hero who has the endurance and forbearance of Job. Yet Morris is more than just a sufferer, more than a victim of circumstances and poor judgment—he is also a good man. Acquainted with the tragic side of life, inured to failure, Morris dignifies suffering by insisting that people must continue to trust each other in the face of their common hardship. An old man who needs his sleep more than he needs three cents, Morris nevertheless drags himself up each morning to wait on the thankless Polish woman. Early in the novel, although near bankruptcy himself, Morris allows the ten-year-old daughter of an alcoholic to buy on credit, a debt he knows he will never collect.

Morris's compassion is matched by his honesty, which is so exacting that at his funeral the rabbi relates that Morris once ran two blocks in the snow to return a nickel to a customer. But while Morris's goodness is a moral asset, it is a financial liability. The soul of honesty himself, he seems destined to trust the wrong people. "He was," his daughter reflects, "Morris Bober and could be nobody more fortunate." In spite of continual disappointment, he steadfastly believes that people are better than they appear through their deeds.

Frank Alpine, on the other hand, is at the outset a shiftless drifter with a sordid past who, the reader feels, is not worthy of Morris's trust. Frank's past is revealed in flashbacks of tortured memories of want and failure blurred by guilt. He is an orphan who was shunted around from one foster home to another and was on the road at fifteen. At one point we learn he had wandered drunk for months, living in gutters and scrounging food from garbage cans. Having drifted into crime by robbing the Bober store, he now seeks to repay Morris by working for him, but through such efforts he succeeds only in increasing and intensifying his guilt.

Frank soon begins to repeat his pattern of failure again. Having vowed to himself to help Morris in every way possible—he even secretly returns the $6.50 he got from the robbery—Frank begins to steal money from the cash drawer. Although tortured by his conscience, Frank continues to steal, feeling "a curious pleasure in his misery." As we are told later, "he was like a man with two minds."

Frank does have, however, some inarticulated aspirations and a kind of inexact goodness that vie with his criminal instincts. He is as much a puzzle to himself as he is to others. His feelings become more snarled because Jews seem as strange to him as he does to the suspicious Ida Bober. He despises Morris for his suffering; at the same time, he forces himself, in an attempt to salve his conscience for his part in the robbery, to share the misery of Morris's existence. Almost against his will, he begins to think and act like Morris. Near the end of the novel, Frank tries to collect an old bill from Carl, an unemployed painter whom he sees buying liquor at the store next door. However, when he goes to Carl's house and sees his poverty, Frank runs back to the store and gets his last $3 to give to Carl's wife. The novel traces the knotty path of Frank's moral growth as he absorbs the goodness of his master and spiritual father, Morris Bober.

From the time of their first meeting, Frank and Morris begin a close relationship, although both refuse to recognize their affinity. Frank gravitates toward the stability of the store. Morris still mourns the loss of his long-dead son, Ephraim, and unconsciously accepts Frank as a surrogate son. After hearing Frank tell the story of his early life, Morris thinks to himself, "Poor boy. . . . I am sixty and he talks like me."

Alternately attracted to and disgusted by Morris's honesty, compassion, and forbearance, Frank comes to associate these qualities with Morris's Jewishness. When he can barely endure his poverty and isolation, Frank tells himself that Morris is able to suffer only

because he is a Jew and Jews live to suffer: he who suffers the most is the best Jew. Slowly, he comes to
respect Morris, and their relationship subtly shifts
from storekeeper and assistant, to father and son, to
teacher and novitiate. One day Frank asks why Jews
suffer so much. Everyone suffers, Morris replies, but
Jews suffer for the law, which means, simply, for
honesty and goodness. Pointing out that other religions
also believe in these principles, Frank asks what Morris
suffers for. "I suffer for you," comes the calm reply.

Morris's statement about suffering makes explicit
the central theme of *The Assistant*: man's inherent
potential of transcending the inevitable pain and
hardship in life by making suffering meaningful. In
Morris Bober we see the quintessential Jewish sufferer,
a Job-like character who suffers simply because it is his
lot in life. Suffering is central to Morris's identity; he
needs it, expects it, and receives it in generous doses.
But suffering is also an essential part of his goodness—if he were not a good man, Malamud implies, he
would not be subject to suffering in such overwhelming onslaughts. Because of his unwavering honesty and
compassionate belief that people are better than they
seem, Morris is doomed to a material suffering that
plays a counterpoint to an arduously won but genuine
spiritual triumph. The affirmative nature of Morris's
travail is dramatized by the transformation of Frank
Alpine, under Morris's influence, from moral degener-
ate to a good man who has accepted another's burden
of suffering out of a commitment to responsibility,
compassion, and nourishing love.

Thematically, the novel turns on a paradox: Morris's failure is his success. The sustained goodness of his
heart in the face of business failure signals his spiritual
achievement. This paradox receives emphasis from the
contrast between Morris and his two Jewish neighbors,
Sam Pearl and Julius Karp. The three Jewish families

live in a small cluster within a gentile neighborhood.
Sam Pearl owns only a small candy store but has made
enough money betting on race horses to send his son to
both college and law school. Julius Karp, who started
as a shoe salesman, becomes rich operating a liquor
store in their poor neighborhood, selling a product
Morris refuses on principle to stock in his own store.
Morris's isolation is complete. He is a Jew in a non-
Jewish neighborhood and a commercial failure surrounded by Jewish success.

Two recurrent motifs are interwoven into the
novel, adding richness of texture to the central idea of
the imprisoning pressures of life; they also amplify the
idea that moral growth and transcendence are possible
through meaningful suffering. The first motif—Saint
Francis of Assisi as moral example—relates especially
to the characterization of Frank Alpine. Many times
during the novel, Frank thinks about Saint Francis,
who gave away his worldly possessions and lived in
poverty with the birds and the flowers. He reads a
book about the saint's life, tells Helen a story about
him, dreams about him. When he first arrives in the
neighborhood, Frank stops in Sam Pearl's candy store
and discovers in a magazine a picture of a "thin-faced,
dark-bearded monk" raising his arms to a flock of
birds. Frank tells Sam how, as a child in an or-
phanage, he used to hear stories about Saint Francis
and still remembers the saint giving away all his
belongings: "poverty was a queen and he loved her like
a beautiful woman." Saint Francis's dedication to
poverty represents Frank's genuine, but still obscure,
ideal.

Malamud keeps the reader aware of Frank's instinctive attraction to Saint Francis by associating
Frank with images of birds, flowers, and trees. Even
when he succumbs to a base desire to spy on Helen in
the shower, Frank sees her naked body as "young, soft,

lovely, the breasts like birds in flight, her ass like a flower." When he tries to make amends to Helen for grossly offending her, Frank fashions out of wood "a rose starting to bloom." After he has confessed to Morris his part in the burglary, Frank's sense of relief is conveyed in the words "a treeful of birds broke into song."

In Morris's self-immolation, Frank senses Saint Francis's gentleness of spirit and associates it with Morris's Jewishness. After being near Morris for some time, Frank feels his rage disappearing and a kind of gentleness stealing into his being. Halfway through the novel, Helen goes for a walk in the park and sees a man feeding pigeons. He is surrounded by birds fluttering around him, landing on him, eating peanuts out of his hand. The man is Frank, and for a moment the reader imagines him as Saint Francis. In the next to the last paragraph of the novel, Frank imagines that the saint becomes his intercessor with Helen (whom he wooed with success for a while but finally offended unforgivably) by retrieving from a garbage can the wooden rose Frank had made for Helen and presenting it to her with a flourish. From Saint Francis she accepts the offering, although it comes with "the love and best wishes of Frank Alpine." This is only a daydream, but it strengthens in the reader's mind Frank's association with the saint and with unselfish, nurturing love.

A second motif—the American Dream of success—operates as an ironic backdrop for the development of the main ideas. As a businessman in the land of opportunity, Morris is a miserable failure. He long ago gave up the dream of success, abandoning plans to attend pharmacy school at night and, instead, accepted the confines of the store. He is a poor businessman with no "get up and go." Such things as profits, expansion, and status are less important to him than satisfying his customers. Pride in his profession rather than the logic of business organization shapes his life, but the social images and dreams of materialistic success—even in his disadvantaged neighborhood—constantly remind Morris that he is a complete failure.

Near the end of the novel, Morris, close to bankruptcy, goes job hunting. After visiting many employment agencies in vain, he sits down exhausted on a waiting-room bench of the last agency on his list but is promptly chased away by an unfriendly manager. On the ground floor of the building he is finally able to rest over coffee at "a dish-laden table in the Automat. America." On his death bed, Morris accepts America's judgment of him: "I gave away my life for nothing." But he did not, for Frank Alpine has absorbed Morris's devotion to an ethic of honesty, compassion, and responsibility that struggles precariously to survive in modern competitive society.

Frank, too, is caught up in the American Dream of success. He has traveled east to begin a new life of crime, we are told, doubtless inspired by Hollywood gangster movies and dime novels. "At crime he would change his luck, make adventure, live like a prince." Later, with the help of a "good woman" (Helen), he settles on a more socially acceptable dream and proudly tells Helen that he is going to go to college to make something of himself. Finally, assuming Morris's ethics, he rejects the dream of materialistic success and achieves spiritual triumph.

The American Dream captures Helen's imagination, as well. Wanting "the higher things in life" (the advantages that come with education, status, and wealth), she envisions a future with her neighbor, Nat Pearl, a promising young law student, only to be wounded by the reality of his shallow materialism and self-centered insensitivity. She fastens on education as a means of improving her position in society, but fails to understand the moral values inherent in the "great books" she reads. When she thinks she is in love with Frank, she confuses the real Frank with the one she dreams about—the one who marries her, goes to graduate school, and settles down with her in a little cottage in California near her retired parents. She even gets him to send away for college bulletins. Because she desires simultaneously the American Dream and a sense of spiritual fulfillment, she loses both, although the novel's ending suggests that she may learn to see the hollowness of her materialistic aspirations.

One of the most striking effects in *The Assistant* is the disparity between the oppressive milieu in which the action takes place and the affirmative moral message. We are presented with an aesthetic paradox that parallels the central thematic one. On the material level, the story is one of defeat, and yet morally and aesthetically it conveys great beauty.

The key to understanding Malamud's accomplishment in creating the world of *The Assistant* lies in his use of Jewish humor. He has adapted Yiddish folk materials and combined them with a double-edged, somewhat absurdist irony to produce a subtle humor that simultaneously sustains optimism and pessimism, a balanced interplay of hope and despair. To begin with, the characterization of Morris Bober contains a crucial element suggested neither by a recounting of the plot nor from a discussion of the themes. Morris is, in fact, as much a comic as a tragic character. The humor centers around Morris as schlemiel. He is like the character from Yiddish folk literature who is repeatedly knocked down by fortune but who always struggles to his feet to try his luck again, hoping for the best but expecting the worst, constantly aware of the absurdity of his situation and his actions in the face of an unlucky fate.

Morris Bober follows in the tradition of the heroes

of Yiddish folktales who mutter to themselves and complain loudly, with ironic self-deprecation, about the difficulties of their lot in life. His neighbor Karp, the owner of the well-stocked liquor store, fears a robbery, but Morris is robbed. Fully aware of the absurdity of his impoverished store being the target of burglars, while Karp's "pleasure palace" stands untouched next door, Morris thinks to himself: "The end fitted the day. It was his luck, others had better." When Morris is tempted to pay a *macher* (someone who knows how to do things) to set a fire in order to collect the insurance, Karp's store burns down for free. "Everything for him who has." When Morris attempts to start a fire alone, his conscience rebels and he accidently sets himself on fire (and is rescued by Frank). Throughout the novel, like the traditional hard-luck character of Yiddish folklore, Morris is the unwitting architect of his own misfortune. Whenever he tries to act out of character—yielding to the demands of the American Dream—he suffers a reversal, always fully aware of the comic incongruity.

In addition to the humor of Morris as schlemiel, *The Assistant* contains a more subtle kind of humor. There is a rich vein of Yiddish humor that presents fantastic or bizarre occurrences as though they were commonplace. Such comic fantasy, although muted, is present in *The Assistant*. One night a skinny, shabbily dressed man with a wisp of red beard appears in front of the counter and offers to solve all of Morris's problems if he has "insurinks" (insurance). "I make fires. . . . Magic. . . . No ashes." Morris sends away this agent of the devil but later succumbs to temptation and tries to execute the plan himself, with comic results. Sneaking into the basement in the middle of the night, he inserts the negatives of some old photographs into a crack between two boards. With shaking hand and muttered self-encouragement, Morris lights the celluloid and watches, as if in a trance, as the flames shoot up the wall. Suddenly horrified by what he is doing, Morris tries to beat out the fire. Discovering that the bottom of his apron is burning, "he smacked the flames with both hands and then his sweater sleeves began to blaze. He sobbed for God's mercy, and was at once roughly seized from behind [by Frank] and flung to the ground."

The special world of *The Assistant* also depends a great deal on Malamud's handling of narrative technique and language, both of which incorporate a considerable amount of Jewish humor. The point of view alternates between objective narration and the interior musings of the characters. It is through the latter that Malamud worked his magic. The private thoughts of the characters come over in a language that subtly fuses elements of Yiddish with the vocabulary and syntax of standard English. In Ida's thoughts, for example, the Yiddish elements are most pronounced, probably to indicate her parochial vision. In Helen's thoughts the Yiddish elements are subdued (because she was born and raised in America) and coexist with big-city colloquialisms, as when she wishes to herself that Frank would get less "hot and bothered" whenever they are alone together.

Malamud's handling of Morris is more complex. Although he speaks in Yiddish dialect when conversing with his wife and other people from the old country, in his thoughts the Yiddish voice is pronounced just enough to associate him with a subculture but without depicting him as an ethnic stereotype. Malamud tells of Morris going for a haircut:

The chair was empty and he didn't have to wait. As Mr. Giannola, who smelled of olive oil, worked on him and they talked, Morris, though embarrassed at all the hair that had to be cut by the barber, found himself thinking mostly of his store. If it would only stay like this—no Karp's paradise, but at least livable, not the terrible misery of only a few months ago—he would be satisfied. Ida had again been nagging him to sell, but what was the use of selling until things all over got better and he could find a place he could have confidence in?

The language has a Yiddish flavor; there is inverted syntax and odd treatment of verbs and verb complements as in Yiddish dialect ("things all over got better"); constant interruptions and interjections of modifiers or qualifiers ("no Karp's paradise, but at least livable") give a faintly Yiddish air; and the final interrogative suggests the Yiddish-speaker's habit of answering a question (Ida's query about selling) with a question ("What was the use of selling. . . ?").

In depicting Frank Alpine, Malamud relies on his handling of point of view rather than language to shape the reader's response to Frank's moral growth. Privy to his innermost thoughts, aspirations, guilts, and conflicts, we see him struggle with his awakening conscience and slowly, gropingly, evaluate himself, reflecting, justifying, and finally gaining a sense of his own morality; we witness a complex process of self-purification. As Frank grows in ethical depth, we see the existential import of intellectual and moral suffering, as well as of the physical suffering in everyday life. The influence of Morris Bober is underscored as we hear, by the end of the novel, a Yiddish voice creeping into Frank's private thoughts.

The distinctive texture of *The Assistant* owes a great deal to Malamud's skillful use of language. He captured in English what has been called an untranslatable quality of Yiddish, a special mixture of irony, comedy, and tragedy that conveys both despair and hope. Much of the dialogue successfully captures the rhythm and flavor of Yiddish dialect, that familiar staple of Jewish comedians. Consider, for example, the following exchange between Morris and his wife:

> "I think I will shovel the snow," he told Ida at lunch-time.
>
> "Go better to sleep."
>
> "It ain't nice for the customers."
>
> "What customers—who needs them?"
>
> "People can't walk in such high snow," he argued.
>
> "Wait, tomorrow it will be melted."
>
> "It's Sunday, it don't look so nice for the goyim that they go to church."

In this brief exchange Malamud brilliantly cap-tures not only the rhythms of Yiddish dialect but also the double vision of Jewish humor. Morris is thinking of others, but his wife wants him to think of himself. When Morris suggests that it is just common sense to keep the sidewalk clear for customers, Ida's response reveals first the bitter awareness that customers are few and far between ("what customers") and then the defensive expectation of misfortune ("who needs them?"). Morris persists in wanting to do something for others. Yet his final line reveals a subtle mixture of attitudes toward Christians—he respects their right to practice their own religion but refers to them as "goyim," that pejorative term with overtones (gained during centuries of Jewish persecution in Europe) of dullness, insensitivity, and heartlessness. And does the phrase "it don't look so nice" contain the added sugges-tion that "the goyim" attach great importance to ap-pearances? In this way Malamud reveals that Morris wishes to help even outsiders whom he disparages at the same time he is being considerate of them. The in-terplay of Morris's implicit optimism with Ida's pessimism is capped by a final, heartrending irony; as a result of his snow-shoveling, Morris catches a severe case of pneumonia and dies. The reader confronts the question, was Ida or Morris right? The double-edged irony evident in the above dialogue balances optimism with pessimism, and ridicules Morris as a schlemiel at the same time that it glorifies him as a moral exemplar.

Other kinds of irony are also present in *The Assistant*, operating at several levels simultaneously (or perhaps in a sequence of levels). The unwinding of the plot contains a series of ironic reversals. The most central of these occurs when Frank is caught stealing from Morris's cash drawer some of the money he has recently slipped in as repayment for his previous pilferage. Partly as a result of this disgrace, Frank loses Helen just as he thinks he has won her.

Another form of irony, a dramatic irony, lies in the disparity between appearances and reality—especially since Frank Alpine is not who he appears to be. Frank parades as an earnest, good-hearted helper just down on his luck, but he is, in fact, the guilt-ridden thief who robbed Morris. Helen and Ida never learn of Frank's secret, so that many of his acts and words have a meaning different to the reader than for the two women. For example, Helen senses something secretive and evasive in Frank but benevolently concludes that this stems from the pain of his childhood. She is flattered that she is helping him to forget the suffering of his past, little realizing that the more she responds to his advances the more his tortured conscience forces him to become even more secretive.

Further ironies stem from the intricacies of the relationship between Jew and Gentile. Although the reader can see that Frank and Morris are almost immediately attracted to each other, each has strong prejudices about the religion of the other that prevents him from enjoying their affinity. Thus the father-son relationship that develops is supremely ironic, for

Frank begins unconsciously to emulate a man he also despises for his long-suffering Jewishness, becoming, in effect, a Christian Jew.

A complex irony of ambiguity finds its focal point in Malamud's treatment of Frank's character. Throughout the novel, Frank demonstrates a masochism that colors every action. Having participated in a shameful robbery and beating, he hangs around the Bober store as much out of a need to punish himself as to "make it up" to Morris. This is clearly revealed when Frank begins slipping money from the cash drawer, feeling "a curious pleasure" in the conscience-stricken misery that results. Frank's masochism is also evident in his relationship with Helen. Drawn to her by the lure of the forbidden as well as by a genuine liking for her (and a vague desire to improve his moral character by association), Frank rages with lust for her at one moment and is filled with tenderness the next. His lust often appears prompted by the self-destructive feelings of self-hate. He climbs the dumbwaiter to spy on her in the shower, all the while aware that his shameful act places her further from his reach, his passion is "poisoned by his shame." Tortured with the thought of her inaccessibility, he saves her from being raped in the park only to rape her himself, and all the while he thinks of her as "beyond his reach, forever in the bathroom as he spied . . ."

As Frank slowly becomes recreated in the image of Morris Bober, his suffering begins to take on meaning; he genuinely tries to make life easier for Helen and her mother. And yet Frank's relationship with suffering remains mixed. Before formally converting to Judaism, Frank has himself circumcised (in biblical reference, this suggests a cleansing of sin) and for a while "dragged himself around with a pain between his legs." This ending clearly reinforces the feeling that Frank's suffering is caused at least in part by his

masochistic tendencies; the ambiguity seems to undercut the novel's moral message of Frank's conversion to
a new way of life. The title, as well, suggests an ironic
ambiguity. Does Frank's new self-identity cast him
forever in the role of apprentice to his predecessor?
Will he always live in the shadow of Morris Bober?

The entire ending is permeated with ambiguity.
Frank has absorbed the goodness and compassion of
his master and spiritual father, but he has also, in a
sense, chosen a life of suffering within the prisonlike
confines of Morris's store. He has assumed the responsibility of providing for Helen's future—at the same
time hoping eventually to regain her love—but we are
left to wonder whether he will ever succeed. Malamud
clearly intended the conclusion to represent a spiritual
victory for Frank Alpine, but the affirmation is riddled
with ambiguities. Doctrine plays little part in Frank's
conversion; Judaism merely provides him with a practical means of enduring the suffering necessary for
salvation. As a Christian Jew, Frank becomes Everyman, exemplifying the fundamental unity of men's
spiritual needs. For Malamud, religion's function is to
convey the essentials of the "good heart"; he has little
sympathy for the ghetto-minded Jew or parochial
Christian.

The ambiguity of the ending points to both the
achievement and the weaknesses of *The Assistant.*
Frank Alpine's conversion to Judaism provides an appropriate action to round out the themes of the novel,
but because *The Assistant* is neither purely natural-
istic, nor existential, nor symbolic, the reader has no
context in which to receive this symbolic action. The
ending is not convincing because no simple literary
device could resolve the underlying tensions. In a
similar fashion, the Saint Francis motif that Malamud
so painstakingly develops functions as a way of univer-
salizing the themes; it appears forced, however, be-

cause it suffers from sentimentality and simply does not work at the emotional level.

The problem is that the real power of *The Assistant* derives not so much from its statement about the regenerative power of meaningful suffering as from the underlying interaction of Morris and Frank as father and son. Frank is an orphan searching for a father; Morris is a sorrowing father seeking an emotional substitute for his dead son. The archetypal core of the novel is a variation of the biblical story of the Prodigal Son, in which the father demonstrates unwavering love for his wayward son. The emotional high point of the novel occurs when Morris reveals that he already has guessed Frank's involvement in the robbery, thus demonstrating that Frank's desire to confess is matched by Morris's desire to forgive. As pat as this revelation might seem at the plot level, it does work emotionally. But Malamud becomes so concerned with embellishing the moral message—clothing it always in ironic camouflage—that he neglects, sometimes even undercuts, the power of the underlying father-son archetype.

In spite of these weaknesses, *The Assistant* is unquestionably a brilliant novel. Malamud weaves an intricate plot, and in taking the reader through unexpected but believable twists and reverses, he proves himself a master of both dramatic and ironic effect. Through an intense observation of the urban setting and a mastery of Yiddish speech rhythms, Malamud captures the color and texture of Jewish immigrant life. Out of the daily aches and indignities of poor people struggling in a search for meaning in a harsh existence, he creates an artistic expression of simple dignity that presents a vision of the life of all men, not just Jews.

The world of *The Assistant* is a world of opposites—optimism and pessimism, hope and despair, humor and pathos, transcendence and entrapment, materialism and morality. All the characters and situations, good and bad alike, are bathed in Malamud's compassion. His vision encompasses human pain and human potential. He conveys hope through the dual vision of Jewish humor; he captures the bitter reality of suffering and shows the possibilities for spiritual growth through such suffering.

# 4

••••••••••••••••••••••••••••••••••••••••••••••••••••••••••

# The Schlemiel Out West:
*A New Life*

Malamud's third novel, *A New Life*, seems far removed from *The Assistant*. Malamud deserts the
timeless, closed-in oppressiveness of Morris Bober's
New York City for the lush groves of a Pacific-
Northwest academe. Seymour Levin, a New York Jew,
"formerly a drunkard," leaves the East to teach
English at Cascadia College in the mythical locale of
Easchester, Cascadia—and begins a new life in the
great American West.

The first half of the novel takes Levin, full of high
hopes about his new career as a college teacher and his
escape from the East (and his old identity as drunkard), through a series of comic misadventures. In the
second half of the story, Levin in a sense begins his
"new life" anew when he is drawn into an illicit love
affair with Pauline Gilley, the wife of the man who
hired him. The affair is intense, but eventually love
and its problems overwhelm Levin. He calls an end to
the affair, and, turning his attention instead to an
attempt to liberalize the English department, he
launches an ill-fated campaign for the department
chairmanship. Levin thus begins another phase of his
new life as an idealist immersed in the sordidness of
departmental intrigue; by the end of the academic
year he succeeds in stirring up "a terrible discord."

Levin's new role as activist within the department
is unexpectedly cut short when he learns from Pauline

that she is unable to give up her love for him. It is
agreed that she will ask her husband for a divorce in
order to be with Levin and have her own life. That
night Levin wakes up in a fright as he senses a figure
standing at the foot of his bed. It is Gerald Gilley, who
offers him a proposition—he will provide good references if Levin will resign and leave Cascadia, alone.
Levin refuses. He is quickly dismissed from his job for
moral turpitude. His dream of a new life is in
shambles. Soon after, he learns that Pauline is pregnant with his child. We last see Levin driving out of
town with a pregnant woman he no longer loves and
her two children.

A New Life is Malamud's first attempt at social
satire, and much of the novel is given over to it. On his
second day in Easchester, Levin learns from Gerald
Gilley, the director of the Freshman English program,
that Cascadia College is not a liberal arts college. He
has, in fact, confused it with Cascadia's other state
university. As Gilley cuts pictures out of Life magazine
for a future "Picture Book of American Lit," he explains that the curriculum at Cascadia College is
geared mostly to science and technology. The English
Department is "service-oriented," having no majors
and offering primarily grammar-oriented composition
courses. Department chairman Fairchild later explains
to Levin that no one ever felled a tree or built a dam
with poetry.

Levin soon discovers that Cascadia College is, in
fact, a monument to mediocrity, an intellectual wasteland where no geniuses are allowed to hang around.
The emphasis is on practical learning, prestige,
grades, legislative approval, and the well-rounded
shallow man who to be accepted must be more an ath-
lete than a scholar. Levin learns to keep his office door
closed while reading and has to fight the impulse to

hide his book whenever someone knocks. As he watches the class in fly-casting across the street, Levin muses, "A new world."

In his introductory interview with the chairman of the department, Orville Fairchild, Levin confronts a man whose idea of a leader is someone who knows how to take orders from his superiors and pass them on to his subordinates. Inordinately conscious of the department's "image," Fairchild is fond of discoursing humorously on such subjects as creeping socialism, the tyranny of the New Deal, and the evils of federal aid to education, proudly proclaiming that Easchester has consistently voted against these insidious threats to Americanism. But his great passion in life is grammar. Author of *The Elements of Grammar* (now in its thirty-first edition), his dying words later in the novel are about the mysteries of the infinitive. The renowned author becomes delightfully ludicrous as he narrates the paper-marking habits of Levin's predecessor, Leo Duffy, who had brought radical ideas to Cascadia. Scandalized at learning that Duffy had thrown away several sets of "ungraded and unrecorded" themes wet by his dachshund on the floor where Duffy did his work, Fairchild unexpectedly interrupts himself to ask Levin where he grades his papers.

Fairchild is what Gerald Gilley (and the America he represents) is doomed to become. Both embody intellectual mediocrity, utilitarian values, bourgeois respectability. Both spell out for Levin the do's and don't's of his new position (all of which Duffy violated): get to know *The Elements* backward and forward, grade all papers promptly and diligently, don't "upset other people's applecarts," don't date students, and don't "prowl among faculty wives."

Cascadia College soon becomes a microcosm of America during the early 1950s, the time of Levin's arrival. It reflects the fear of the country at a time when "the cold war blew on the world like an approaching glacier" and when, in the background, "Senator McCarthy held in his hairy fist everyman's name."

Although social satire is prominent in *A New Life*, the novel contains much more: a comedy, a Western adventure, a love story, and an initiation rite. Central to all of these elements is the characterization of the protagonist. Sy Levin is a comic bumbler whose search for a meaningful life is continually thwarted by the interplay of his idealistic, naive wit with an inner sense of guilt and self-hate.

Levin's comic misadventures, bordering on farce, begin almost as soon as he arrives in Easchester. While eating dinner at the Gilleys' he has tuna cassarole dumped in his lap and later makes their little boy laugh so uncontrollably by bouncing him on his lap and making up stories that he becomes soaked by a sticky stream of urine. "I've got to get out," he thinks, "before they hate me." On the first day of class Levin receives rapt attention as he stands to welcome the class, reaching for the lofty heights of oratory, only to look down "as if inspired" to discover his fly "all the way open."

Although Levin wants very much to succeed in his new career, it is not long before he finds himself violating, one by one, the injunctions cited by his superiors. Against his better judgment, Levin succumbs to the charms of Nadalee, a seductive student who initiates a liaison with her instructor. In a hilarious episode, Levin, who has not quite finished teaching himself to drive, rushes to a rendezvous by the sea with his Lady of the Lake, who earlier wrote an essay about the virtues of nude swimming. Before leaving, he pictures himself as a knight speeding over hill and dale in his trusty Hudson, on his way to a series of "amorous and philanthropic adventures."

52                                              Bernard Malamud

After having car trouble, encountering inpenetrable
fog, meeting a mysterious old man who gives the
wrong directions, and being forced into a ditch by a
gigantic logging truck, Levin is rescued by a wizened
old farmer. This "purgatorial journey" that seems to
extend endlessly on an abandoned road finally ends
when Levin sees the ocean. Feeling like "stout Cor-
tez—Balboa that is," he stumbles exhaustedly into
Nadalee's arms.

The affair turns sour almost before it begins.
Within a few days he realizes he never felt any affection for the girl. His chivalric spirit is depressed by the
thought that he won her only by taking advantage of
his position as a teacher. Disenchanted with his
students and laid low by a miserable cold in the deep
of winter, Levin sinks into the depths of despair.
Lamenting that his "escape to the West" has been
ruined by "the past-contaminated self," he lacerates
himself mercilessly with the memory of "each disgust-
ing defeat" since boyhood and his continuing failure to
master himself. He is frightened by a "crawling self-
hatred" that he thought he had left three thousand
miles behind. Now, he thinks, he can no longer expect
the promise of a new life to be fulfilled.

He initiates his affair with Pauline Gilley when he
inadvertently comes across her in a nearby forest.
Afterward he tells Pauline about his life as a drunk, a
life of utter degradation. After two years of living with
the most intense self-hatred, Levin explains, he under-
went a mystical experience, discovering that life is
holy. Slowly picking up the pieces of his shattered life,
Levin went back to college for a master's degree and
then became a high school teacher. But in order to
really begin a new life, he felt he should leave New
York. In telling Pauline about the humiliation of his
past, Levin indicates a willingness to enter into a
deeper human relationship. But Pauline is the wife of

his immediate superior and the mother of two young children. Although he tells himself that the affair is a matter of convenience, not romance, he cannot escape feelings of guilt and develops an excruciating pain that cripples him sexually. It is, he believes, "the price of emission, a fiery pain in the ass." After a while he avoids sleeping with Pauline. At the same time he becomes disgusted with himself, thinking that this unpleasant situation is "pure Levin, for every pleasure, pain." Levin suffers until he decides that the cause of his pain is "love ungiven." The remedy, he concludes, is to give what he "unwillingly withheld." He plunges wildly in love with Pauline.

Such a romantic love, however, cannot long continue for Levin. After his landlady finds out that Pauline has been coming to his room, and after Pauline's infidelity is nearly discovered by her husband, they begin to see much less of each other, until finally he stops seeing her altogether, telling himself that he must give her up because he loves her. The truth is that he avoids her out of fear that his life will go off in directions he never expected. Months later he receives a letter from Pauline asking to see him. At first he refuses; concluding that he has gone through great suffering in order to free her from suffering, he continues to avoid her. Pauline eventually traps him and confesses her continuing love for him. Levin receives the announcement in silent despair, realizing that he has succeeded in killing his love for her. After this confrontation, Levin tries to recapture his love for Pauline. He decides that because of his former actions he has a responsibility to love her, "without or despite feeling."

The themes of A New Life grow naturally out of the characterization of its protagonist. Levin hopes to find self-fulfillment by beginning a new life far away from the scene of his past defeats, but during much of

the novel he merely repeats his old mistakes. His problem is an inability to learn from his own experiences;
he cannot escape his past. Early in the novel he reflects
on "how past-drenched present time was" and ob-
serves that the past never really disappears. At one
point he copies into his notebook under "insights":
"The new life hangs on an old soul," and, "I am one
who creates his own peril."

In the climactic scene of the novel, however,
Levin is able to transcend his past by passing a trial by
love. On Pauline's behalf, Levin goes to Gilley to ask
for custody of the children. Gilley warns Levin that in
marrying Pauline he will marry a woman "born dissat-
isfied," full of unending complaints about the emp-
tiness of her life and her failure to become "a better
person than she is." Failing to dissuade Levin, Gilley
desperately bargains to retain custody of his children.
Apparently reasoning that Levin could not afford to
accept his conditions, Gilley agrees to allow Levin and
Pauline to have custody if Levin will promise never
again to teach at a college. Asking himself "what else
could I expect given who I am?" Levin agrees. As-
tounded, and knowing that a "fanatic" like Levin will
keep his word, Gilley asks Levin what he is going to do
with an undependable older woman, two adopted
kids, and no prospect of a job. "Why take that load on
yourself?" "Because I can, you son of a bitch." With
that one brief but powerful line, Levin chooses responsibility and defeat. He at last goes beyond carnal
love—"the self again betrayed by the senses"—to commitment and self-sacrifice for the idea of love.

One of Levin's final thoughts in the novel is that
he is trapped in a windowless prison, constructed out
of his doubts and his failures. Everyone, Malamud
seems to be saying, is destined to suffer. It is part of
man's condition. In choosing "to stick it out chained to
her [Pauline's] ribs," Levin insists on the freedom to

choose his own prison and to make his suffering meaningful.

Ironically, Levin's fortunes—good and bad—
turn out to be less a matter of his own doing than he at
first realizes. His application to teach at Cascadia College was picked out of a discard pile by Pauline—because his picture reminded her of a Jewish boy she
once knew who was kind to her (and, the reader
suspects, because Levin reminds her of Duffy). As a
result of being "chosen," Levin, like the Old Testament Jews, must undergo suffering.

Many critics find *A New Life* seriously marred by
a divided intention. Ruth Mandel effectively represents this view when she declares that Levin's personal
life and his public life are not thematically related:

Obviously Malamud is concerned with social comment, with
satirizing the state of Cascadia and especially its College. Obvious also is Malamud's intention to write a novel about a
man in search of love, identity, a set of values. . . . The comic and satiric elements do not function thematically in relation to the novel's serious theme. Levin's ultimate sacrifice
and affirmation really have nothing to do with his experiences as English instructor at the College.[1]

Such reservations are perhaps justified. Yet the two
aspects of the novel have more thematic connections
than are usually acknowledged. They are joined
together by Levin's greatest problem, his romanticism.
Before he can truly engage in life, he must overcome,
or at least modify, his idealized notions about love, the
West, nature, and liberalism.[2] In his flight westward,
Levin has sought to escape the miseries of life by blam-
ing them on the progress of civilization.

Immersed in the writings of Emerson, Thoreau,
and Whitman, Levin believes wholeheartedly the
metaphors about America as a New-World Garden of
Eden. By going west he feels he can recapture his lost

innocence and escape the past—become the New-
World Adam. Discovering that the pioneering spirit is
dead in Cascadia, Levin tells himself that nature itself
provides Easchester's true glory. Awestruck by the
area's natural wonders, he even at one point imagines
himself as "a latter day Thoreau"; in fact, however, he
learns about nature from a picture book, *Western
Birds, Trees and Flowers*, which he has brought with
him from New York. He soon discovers that rain, not
sun, is Cascadia's natural element, and he finds that
when walking in pastures he inevitably stumbles into
brambles and steps in piles of cow dung. In his dreams
he must listen to a gigantic salmon cry "Levin, go
home." By the end of the novel he learns his lesson and
remarks that a beautiful country is fine if "beauty isn't
all that happens."

Levin's idealism is as romantic as his vision of
nature. As he tells Pauline, his emergence from
drunkenness began with a mystical vision that caused
him to become "a man of principle." He firmly
believes that a man's value is determined by his willingness to support his ideals. He has come to subscribe
passionately to the ideals of democracy, humanism,
liberalism (and the liberal arts), freedom, art, and intellect. But his ideals come from his reading and are
not tempered by social experience. His failure as a
liberal—as Gilley recognizes—is caused largely because Levin assumes that his way of thinking is correct
and pushes it on others without trying to understand
how Cascadians think. "I worry," he says to one of his
teaching colleagues, "I'm not teaching how to keep
civilization from destroying itself." His problem is not
knowing how to translate this idealistic purpose into
practice.

Among his colleagues, Levin finds several idealists, all of whom have failed to bring reform to
Cascadia. Each of them is a kind of father figure

representing alternative paths Levin might follow. C. D. Fabricant is the resident scholar with a reputation for intellectual achievement. Levin at first finds him very appealing and turns to him, as an alternative to Gilley, as replacement for the retiring Fairchild. But Levin comes to realize that the life of C. D. is one of complete noninvolvement. He is not married, works always behind a closed door, plays no policy-making role in the affairs of the department, and refuses to commit himself for fear of jeopardizing his anticipated promotion. Joseph Bucket, perhaps the most attractive character in the novel, is a conscientious fellow-instructor with a quick wit and a winning sense of humor. He has a large family to support and a thrice-rejected doctoral dissertation to revise. His outside responsibilities prevent him from risking more than a minor commitment to the cause of reform.

Finally, there is Levin's predecessor, Leo Duffy, who is cited by both Gilley and Fairchild as the example not to follow. Although he never actually appears, the flamboyant Irishman is one of the most important characters in *A New Life*. The myth of Duffy as liberal (radical in the context of Cascadia) permeates the entire novel. Unlike the intellectually sterile Gilley, Duffy was a man of vitality in mind and body. The "official" view of Duffy is challenged by Pauline Gilley, who tells Levin that "Leo" was a genuine idealist who irritated people because he unflinchingly challenged their most dearly held assumptions.

When she tells Levin that Duffy used to say that "a good cause is the highest excitement," Levin writes down the words so he won't forget them. Levin's choosing to become a candidate for department chairman signals his choice of Duffy as spiritual father. Levin learns the necessity of involvement first in the public sector, then in the private. Only after he learns to act upon his convictions with his efforts to improve the English Department at Cascadia College can he agree to marry Pauline and assume the duties of a father.

Duffy is Levin's predecessor in more ways than one, functioning as a parallel and contrast to Levin. Both are idealists, both are radical in the context of Cascadia College, both have an affair with Pauline Gilley, both are fired for moral turpitude. Duffy's efforts at reform had failed miserably because his methods were too flamboyant and antagonistic. Unable to accept the defeat of liberalism, Duffy subsequently killed himself, leaving behind a note that read: "The time is out of joint. I'm leaving the joint."

Levin, too, fails in the department, although his efforts do result in the removal of *The Elements* after its thirty years of domination. Levin learns more about himself than Duffy did. He has undoubtedly learned, although he does not articulate it, the lesson that in the real world efforts at doctrinaire reform are futile. Similarly, the novel upholds the view that romantic notions of love are not enough to sustain a lasting relationship. Levin's love for Pauline is, perhaps, not dead; it merely assumes a new, nonromantic appearance. He has "fallen out of love," but has not necessarily stopped loving.

Malamud's technique for revealing Levin's excessive romanticism reveals the comic and ironic vision of *A New Life* and provides thematic unity as well. Early in the novel Levin manages to arrange to make love to a waitress one night in her uncle's barn. " 'Your breasts,' he murmured 'smell like hay.' 'I always wash well,' she said." His head filled with Emerson, Thoreau, and Whitman, Levin thinks, "In front of the cows. . . . Now I belong to the ages." Just then a jealous rival runs off with their clothes, forcing them to walk three miles to town in bare feet and a horse blanket. Here, as throughout the novel, the ironic con-

trast between Levin's aspirations and their consequences is used for comic effect.

Often the contrast is between Levin's thoughts
and his actions. This technique reinforces the point of
view Malamud develops. The story is told by an om-
niscient narrator, but because Levin is the only
character whose interior thoughts are revealed, great
emphasis is placed upon his fantasies, aspirations,
guilt, and rationalizations. Levin's ironic turn of mind
reveals, through interior monologue as well as exterior
actions, comic discrepancies between his intentions
and their results.

Although *A New Life* is set in a non-Yiddish
milieu, Levin is portrayed as a schlemiel hero. Instead
of the rhythms of Yiddish, Malamud here used the
language of the liberal idealist and the naive romantic,
but the result is similar: Levin is a buffoon destined to
be a material failure but a moral success. Like Don
Quixote who, as an old man, became an absurd and
ineffectual knight errant in a vain attempt to restore
the ideals of a past age, Levin tries to overcome the
flaws of the modern world with the enthusiastic sensibility peculiar to nineteenth-century romanticism.
He is a comic hero whose excesses stem from a misguided but genuine desire to find a place for his ideals
in the real world.

Unlike Don Quixote, however, who suffers from a
temporary delusion, Levin's source of misfortune is his
character. His naivete is counterbalanced by his self-
hate and a highly developed conscience; his comic
adventures are thus accompanied by inner lacerations.
While Don Quixote acts like a fool, Levin *is* a fool, and
unlike Don Quixote he is fully aware of the ironic
discrepancy between the loftiness of his ideals and the
ignominy of his failures. His foolhardiness is revealed
through a double-edged irony that affirms his moral
instincts at the same time that it mocks his social and

personal ineptitude. For example, when he arranges a
rendezvous with his student, Nadalee, Levin hopes to
find true love and an end to loneliness, but after
becoming hopelessly lost on the way to the ocean, he
reflects that "it served him right for his evil intentions." After spending a happy weekend with her,
Levin worries so much about the clandestine affair being discovered that he can no longer enjoy being with
Nadalee. Like the traditional schlemiel, Levin expects
disaster while hoping for a change in his fortune. In
this way, Malamud creates a humor that fuses optimism and pessimism.

Much of the material in *A New Life* is drawn
from Malamud's own experience at Oregon State College in Corvallis, Oregon, where he taught English
from 1949 until 1961. A fascinating essay in *Bernard
Malamud: A Collection of Critical Essays* traces the
parallels between Levin's experiences and Malamud's
own. Like Levin, Malamud was a New Yorker who
was previously a high school teacher. He was assigned
to teach four sections of English Composition in a
rigidly supervised program that emphasized the study
of grammar, punctuation, spelling, and diction. Oregon State, like Cascadia College, was a small, tech-
nically oriented land-grant institution. According to
the essay, "Malamud taught composition at Oregon
State for more than a decade, and he endured the
drudgeries of the department 'theme room' (where all
student papers were filed), grading 'technical reports,'
and monitoring group final examinations in composition with at least a passive tolerance."[3] During his stay
in Oregon, Malamud wrote *The Natural*, *The Assistant*, and his award-winning volume of short stories,
*The Magic Barrel*. When he left, he was internation-
ally famous. Yet because he had no doctoral degree, he

was only occasionally permitted to teach courses in literature.

Although Malamud uses the Northwest and Cascadia College metaphorically, their descriptions bear the unmistakable stamp of real observation. The early scenes beautifully capture the bland informality of a third-rate college and the pompous self-seriousness of a highly organized English composition program. The blending of comedy, satire, and pathos is most effective in those scenes that present Levin's reactions to the vastness and lushness of the Northwest. The novel beautifully captures the incredulous wonder of a man whose previous experience with nature was limited to city parks and an occasional trip to the beach at Coney Island.

And yet, many critics point out that the satire fails to support the real concern of the novel—the world of Levin's inner life, his dual search for self and love. The problem, however, is not that the satire becomes too generalized and stereotyped, as is usually suggested, but rather the opposite. The satire becomes too heavy because Malamud knows too much about the workings of the college. Perhaps he included so much satire and farce in order to release his own pent-up feelings about what must have been a very stultifying time in his life. In any case, Malamud's satire becomes too detailed in giving the behind-the-scenes view, drawing attention away from the main themes. Levin himself is less interesting in the English Department scenes, often hemming and hawing foolishly. We feel for Levin the man but frequently find Levin the professor rather dull.

An even more serious criticism is that the characterization of Levin is inadequate for a full realization of Malamud's vision in *A New Life*. For one thing, it is hard to believe that the Levin we see—a

naive man of conscience—was ever a drunkard. Moreover, a good deal of the humor in the novel, especially
in the more farcical episodes, stems neither from
Levin's idealism nor his conscience. Levin's love trysts,
for example, produce comic consequences, but this
results from just plain bad luck as often as from in-
terferences by his conscience.

Despite its weaknesses *A New Life* is an estimable
novel; in fact, it is one of this writer's personal
favorites. Insofar as it records the misadventures of a
luckless bumbler, the schlemiel in love or out West, *A
New Life* is not just hilarious, but moving and true.
Levin as schlemiel blends into Levin as the dude or
tenderfoot who can never even learn the language
much less the ground rules that govern the strange territory in which he finds himself. The underlying fable,
as critic Leslie Fiedler says, is based on a touching and
comic "account of two provincialities meeting head-on
in a kind of mutual incomprehension which makes
tragedy impossible, since the greatest catastrophe
which can eventuate is a pratfall."[4] Although lacking
the emotional power of *The Assistant*, the comic inventiveness of *A New Life*, its ironic deflation of
romantic idealism and its delightful satire of academic
life, constitute a significant literary achievement.

# 5

●●●●●●●●●●●●●●●●●●●●●●●●●●●●●●●●●●●●●●●●●●●●●●●●●●●●●●●●

# Alienation and Aggression:
## *The Fixer*

*The Fixer* represents for Malamud both a departure and a return to familiar territory. It picks up the major themes of *The Assistant*. The protagonist, Yakov Bok, seeks a new life; he is an unwilling Jew who does not believe in God and who wishes to enjoy the freedoms of Gentiles. Here the setting shifts from 1950s America to tsarist Russia, and the details of the plot loosely parallel those of an actual historical incident, the infamous Mendel Beiliss case.

This is the least complex of Malamud's novels and the plot the most straightforward. Yakov Bok, a Jewish handyman in prerevolutionary Russia, abandons his religious tradition and the hope that his childless wife will return to him, leaves his shtetl (native village) and settles in the city of Kiev, where he hides his identity in order to live and work illegally outside the Jewish ghetto. He is arrested and charged with murdering a Christian boy to use his blood in making Passover matzos. More than three-quarters of the novel is spent in portraying Bok's stubborn endurance through two and a half years in brutal pretrial imprisonment; the novel ends as the trial is about to begin.

Bok is another of Malamud's poor Jews whose life seems to be an unending struggle to make ends meet. "If there's a mistake to make," he thinks, "I'll make it." Somewhat of a schlemiel, who is conscious of his role as loser, Yakov expects calamity and resolves to hold up under it. His speech and reflections are laced with wry Yiddish irony. Deserted by his wife who could bear him no children, barely able to earn enough at odd jobs to live on, Yakov nonetheless is unwilling to accept his status as born loser; thus he resolves to break out of the prison of the shtetl, "an island surrounded by Russia." Only his father-in-law, Shmuel—an old Jew who complains about the hardship of life but who remains faithful to God—is present to wish him well as he departs with his few belongings for Kiev. "Don't forget your God," Shmuel warns. "Who forgets who?" comes the bitter reply. Shmuel continues agitatedly, reminding Yakov that the Jews are surrounded by enemies and must stay under God's protection. "Remember, if he's not perfect, neither are we."

During the early portions of the novel, Malamud emphasizes the theme of denial of identity. Driving an old wagon pulled by a broken-down old nag with rotten teeth, Yakov begins a physical as well as a spiritual journey. The nag's erratic starting and stopping rouses Yakov's intense but feebly misdirected anger: "I'm a bitter man, you bastard horse." Later he beats the horse, thinking, "like an old Jew he looks." At the Dnieper River, Yakov trades the horse for a boat ride, and is ferried by a Charon-like boatman with a shaggy beard and bloodshot eye. Here for the first time Yakov hears of the widespread folk belief that fanatical Jews murder Christian boys as part of their cabalistic rites. Terrified by the hatred of his Jew-baiting pilot, Yakov unobtrusively lets his bag of prayer implements (phylacteries and prayer shawl) slide into the icy water.

In Kiev, Yakov seeks to change his fortune. He rents a room in the Podol, the Jewish district, and looks for work. The Podol is already full of people searching for jobs that do not exist. So Yakov begins seeking employment outside the ghetto, hoping that he may have better luck among the Gentiles. In any case, he reasons, his chances could not be worse.

One night Yakov finds a drunken man lying unconscious in the snow—a fat, bald, prosperous-looking Russian who wears the Double Eagle emblem of the virulently anti-Semitic organization, Black Hundreds. In Good Samaritan fashion, Yakov rescues the man, who later rewards him with a job redecorating part of his house. Yakov's new benefactor, Lebedev, is a wealthy drunkard who speaks in pious platitudes and biblical phrases. Like Chaucer's nun (who is quoted in the novel's opening epigraph), Lebedev weeps over the death of a dog one moment and persecutes Jews the next. Yakov conceals his Jewishness and finally accepts a well-paying job as foreman in Lebedev's brickworks.

Yakov's new position forces him to live in an area of the city forbidden to Jews and, as a kind of overseer-policeman, to antagonize his coworkers. Thus, when the catalytic event occurs—the murder of a Christian boy and the discovery of his body mutilated by thirty-seven stab wounds—all the forces of potential destruction threaten to descend on Yakov's vulnerable head. According to an expert from the Kiev Anatomical Institute, the boy had had his blood drained, "possibly for religious purposes." Yakov's identity is revealed, and he is arrested for the crime.

In tsarist Russia, Jews were forced to live apart from Russians and were treated as an inferior people. Special laws relegated them to a position beneath peasants politically and socially. Jews were subjected to retaliatory mass violence (pogroms) if they offended their Russian neighbors (similar to the "lynch mob law" once used in the American South to keep blacks in their "place"). Ironically, in trying to escape the limitations that his Jewishness imposes on him, Yakov is charged with a crime that assumes a preposterously fanatic Jewish orthodoxy. He becomes a convenient target for the leaders of a despotic government who hope to divert popular discontent away from the government and onto the Jews as scapegoats.

During the rest of the novel, Yakov remains in prison while incriminating circumstantial evidence is found. Two previous incidents in particular are used against him, and both demonstrate the impossibility of escape from his own Jewish conscience. The first occurred when Lebedev's crippled daughter, Zina, made sexual advances to Yakov. After some hesitation, Yakov responded, partly out of pity for the girl, but could not bring himself to continue when he found that she was menstruating and hence, by Jewish law, was "unclean." Later, the angry and humiliated girl publicly accuses Yakov of assaulting her.

The second incident occurred when Yakov once again performed a simple act of human kindness. He found an old Jew one night who had been stoned by malicious boys and was lost and bleeding; Yakov bandaged his head and hid him for the rest of the night in his room. Later, after his arrest, the bloody shirt Yakov used for the bandage and the old man's bag of matzos are found in his room and used as evidence of Yakov's involvement in a conspiracy of Jewish fanatics who are said to use Christian blood in their cabalistic ceremonies.

Yakov's imprisonment introduces several new characters. The principal antagonist is prosecuting attorney Grubeshov, procurator of the Kiev superior court. He gathers evidence, real or imaginary, and combines it in novel ways, twisting reality to suit his own political bias. He continually tries to browbeat Yakov into "confessing." Working for Grubeshov is Father Anastasy of the Orthodox church, a self-proclaimed "specialist" on Judaism.

In a shocking scene, the investigators drag Yakov to the cave where the body was found. Father

Anastasy recites a long "history of Jewish uses for Christian blood," and concludes by insisting that the existence of a fanatic Jewish bloodlust is revealed by the very frequency of the accusations against Jews. Yakov can only cry out in disbelief, "It's all a fairy tale, every bit of it. Who could ever believe such a thing?" He cannot cope with the irrational forces around him. He is still convinced that if he could logically explain to his tormentors what kind of a person he is, he could convince them that he is incapable of such an act, and they would realize they have the wrong man.

Fortunately, not everyone is against Yakov. The investigating magistrate for Cases of Extraordinary Importance, B. A. Bibikov, is a humane and rational man who vows to help see that justice is done. While Yakov spends his first Passover in jail, Bibikov begins gathering evidence to clear him of the charge.

During the second part of the novel, after Yakov's arrest and imprisonment, Malamud focuses the major themes by weaving into the plot references to the philosophy of Spinoza. Somewhat implausibly, Yakov is represented as having developed a passion for reading the works of the great philosopher, alone at night in his cottage in the shtetl. He does not understand all the intricate twists of Spinoza's thought, but he does have an intuitive grasp of the major premises. In his initial interview with Bibikov, Yakov discovers that his learned counsel also has a fondness for Spinoza. Yakov explains that he admires Spinoza because he wanted to make himself free and independent by "thinking things through and connecting everything up." From Spinoza, Yakov learned the central condition of existence—"that life could be better than it is," and that the only way to improve the quality of life is for all men to strive for good will among men, to be reasonable, or else "what's bad gets worse."

Several weeks after the first meeting, Bibikov
visits Yakov in his cell and tells him that the real
murderer is the boy's mother, Marfa Golov, who is involved with a gang of thieves. Grubeshov, he says, also
knows the identity of the real murderer, but finds it
more expedient to accuse a Jew. The only hope of getting the truth out, Bibikov says, is by going to the
press. "So that's how it is," sighs Yakov, "behind the
world lies another world." Yakov had forgotten Spinoza's decree that there is no escape from involvement
in the world. As Yakov himself said to Bibikov, "all
things fit together underneath." Even false accusations
fit into the larger scheme of things; lies remain until
disproved. This conversation marks the beginning of
Yakov's rational and meaningful resistance against his
enemies, and it occurs just in time, for Bibikov is de-
nounced and himself thrown into the solitary cell next
to Yakov's. A few days later he hangs himself.

For all Grubeshov's cleverness at manipulating
facts, he is unable to make a believable case out of the
charge of ritual murder, and so he continually delays
Yakov's indictment. For two and a half years Yakov is
kept in solitary confinement. He is brutalized and
dehumanized, experiencing beatings, hunger, poison,
rats, numbing cold, insanity. Always there is worse to
come. Twice a day he must submit himself to a humiliating search. Soon he is searched six times a day—and
he is kept in chains the rest of the time.

Unexpectedly, Yakov is offered a way to escape
his suffering. If he signs a confession, he can go free.
He refuses because he knows that his confession will be
used against the Jews. Yakov comes to realize that suffering is part of life, but a man can choose to make his
suffering meaningful. Yakov chooses to suffer more so
that others will suffer less. It is this awareness that
leads Yakov to his greatest triumph. Grubeshov offers
Yakov a new opportunity for freedom. The tsar has

agreed to grant certain classes of criminals, including Yakov, amnesty. But Yakov does the unimaginable, he refuses—because he is to be pardoned as a criminal rather than freed as an innocent man. The gesture is absurd but magnificent, an affirmation of his personal dignity and moral integrity. This emotional high point of the novel inspires the reader at the same time that it defeats Yakov's enemies.

Finally the long-awaited indictment comes and with it a lawyer, Julius Ostrovsky, who informs Yakov of Shmuel's death, of the worldwide attention his case has received, and of the mounting evidence against Marfa Golov. Through Ostrovsky, Malamud explains how Yakov's case "relates underneath" to "the frustrations of recent Russian history." "I'm only one man, what do they want from me?" Yakov asks. Ostrovsky tells him that they only need one man to create an example of Jewish bloodlust. "You suffer for us all."

After Ostrovsky leaves, Yakov comes to the conclusion that "what happens to somebody starts a web of events outside the personal." He recalls that Ostrovsky told him that Russia suffers from much more than its anti-Semitism. "Those who persecute the innocent were themselves never free." In his sleep, Yakov dreams that Bibikov comes and tells him that "the purpose of freedom is to create it for others"; Yakov answers that something inside him has changed and he is not the same person he once was. A major irony of *The Fixer* is that Yakov Bok learns what freedom is by enduring a nearly intolerable imprisonment.

In the final pages of the novel, the miracle of Yakov's spiritual victory begins to emit a holy aura. When the deputy warden refuses to release Yakov to the soldiers who have come to escort him to his trial, the guard Kogin intervenes. Yakov is released, but Kogin is shot in the scuffle. He has sacrificed himself in order to insure that Yakov will finally receive justice.

The novel closes with Yakov riding in a carriage to his trial. The ending leaves the outcome of Yakov's case in doubt, but the verdict is really irrelevant to the main concerns of the novel, for Yakov has already achieved the understanding of freedom he envied in Spinoza. This point is underscored in the closing scene. A young Cossack rides as escort alongside the carriage that takes Yakov to his trial. Yakov envies him his youth, his good looks, his freedom. Suddenly, a bomb goes off and the Cossack's foot is blown away. "He looked in horror and anguish at Yakov as though to say, 'What has my foot got to do with it?' " The answer is that the youth is no more free than Yakov. All things connect underneath. Yakov has an inner freedom his oppressors lack. Malamud develops this paradox so powerfully that the memory of Yakov Bok is likely to inspire the reader long after he has finished reading the story.

Because such a great portion of *The Fixer* is devoted to Yakov's solitary suffering, Malamud faced the difficult artistic problem of preventing the story from becoming static. One solution was to introduce Yakov's fantasy life. As Bok's mental anguish pushes him to the edge of sanity, he has a series of fantastic hallucinations in which he is accused of murder and cruelty by a child singing with his throat slit, by "a bloody horse with frantic eyes," and by the image of little Zhenia Golov, the murdered boy. Yakov even fantasizes a pogrom in which he sees childhood friends from his orphan home.

Malamud also effectively uses a variety of stylistic techniques. He sets up a contrast between the language of the official proceedings—formal and pretentious—and the natural simplicity of Yakov's own speech. This effect is heightened by the incongruity between what is said by the investigators and what is transpiring in Yakov's mind. Cleverly, Malamud consummates this effect by having Yakov reply to his persecutors in the same stilted and officious manner they employ. This emphasizes Yakov's lack of fluency in Russian (Yiddish is his native language) and also serves to reinforce the moral division of evil Russians against good Jews. The humor stemming from Malamud's use of Yiddish dialect also helps enliven *The Fixer* and prevents it from becoming unbearably gloomy. The dream sequences of feverish fantasy counterpoint the flat, understated style used in much of the novel. In this way the style accomplishes the double task of lightening the burden of suffering while avoiding excessive sentimentality.

By skillfully weaving into the narrative several different symbolic parallels to the events of Yakov's life, Malamud creates a heightened sense of universality. He has said of *The Fixer* that "it has to be treated as a myth, an endless story more than a case study. A case study couldn't be art."[1] Beneath the surface details of *The Fixer*'s depiction of injustice and spiritual triumph, one can discern the outlines of a mythic theme found frequently in Greek literature and in the folklore of many cultures, namely, the search for a father. Yakov Bok is an orphan unconsciously seeking a spiritual father. Moreover, he would like to be a father himself, and he acts coldly toward his wife because she bears him no children. One possible father figure (and thus moral example) for Yakov is the tsar, a father to his people, with whom Yakov often talks in his dreams. Sometimes addressing him as Little Father, Yakov even discusses the problems the tsar has with his hemophiliac son. Yakov rejects him as spiritual model, however, because of the tsar's support of repression and injustice.

Yakov's spiritual growth is reflected in his changing attitude towards two other father figures. After he has been in prison for quite awhile, a guard, Kogin,

begins telling Yakov his troubles with his son, a potential criminal. At first Yakov listens out of boredom, but
slowly he begins to offer real sympathy to this man he
once considered his oppressor. A similar softening
takes place in his attitude toward his father-in-law,
Shmuel. At first resentful of him for having faith in
God yet bringing up a faithless daughter, Yakov's
resentment slowly changes to compassion. Late in the
novel, Yakov is so lost in despair that he contemplates
suicide. Then one night he dreams that Shmuel has
died, and he awakens crying out, "Live, Shmuel, . . .
live. Let me die for you. . . . if I must suffer let it be
for something. Let it be for Shmuel."

As Yakov's inhuman ordeal miraculously begins
to result in spiritual growth, a biblical parallel
becomes apparent: in the story of Yakov, Malamud
parallels many of the incidents in the life of Christ.
Just as Jesus must go to Jerusalem to suffer, Yakov
enters Kiev, "the Jerusalem of Russia," also situated on
three hills. There he reenacts the parable of the Good
Samaritan. Later, when Yakov is in jail, a guard gives
him a copy of the New Testament to read. He is
fascinated by the story of Jesus, "a strange Jew,
humorless and fanatic," and is deeply moved by his
suffering. What especially impresses Yakov is the vision of Jesus hanging on the cross crying to God for
help; he prefers this to the more comfortable image of
Jesus accepting his injustice and forgiving his execu-
tioners with the words, "Father forgive them for they
know not what they do," in Luke 23:35. In this way
Malamud is able to draw attention to Yakov's role as
scapegoat while at the same time emphasizing his existential anguish.

Through his reading of the New Testament,
Yakov discovers the irony of his situation. How can
people who believe Christ's teachings keep others suffering in prison? He astonishes the guard Kogin by ask-

ing the same question Christ asked his accusers: "Which of you convicts me of sin? . . . If I tell the truth why do you not believe me?" Later he is chained to the wall with arms outstretched, like Christ on the cross. The symbolism is appropriate, for Yakov has become an archetypal scapegoat. He is aware that he acts not for himself alone but for a whole people. Yet Malamud is not implying that Yakov has become a kind of Christ figure whose suffering will redeem the sins of others. He uses the parallel ironically as a way of giving a moral perspective that is not specifically Christian.

For example, asked by the tsar in the final dream sequence whether suffering has not taught him the meaning of mercy, Yakov replies that the main thing his suffering has taught him is the uselessness of suffering. At the conclusion of this dream, Yakov shoots the tsar with a revolver that magically appears in his hand: "Better him than us." Yet these uncharitable thoughts and actions occur only in Yakov's mind; in his actions throughout his imprisonment he emerges as something of a saint. During Yakov's final imaginary conversation with him, the tsar insists that he is a kind person who loves his people, including the Jews. Yakov, however, condemns the tsar to death for failing to rule with justice and mercy. The implied conclusion is obvious: thoughts and intentions are not the most important measure of a man's character. Yakov's actions establish him as a saintly person, just as the tsar's official actions patently prove him a cruel agent of injustice.

Malamud creates one further biblical parallel that is central to his vision in *The Fixer*. Yakov is kin to Job, the archetypal suffering Jew; however, Yakov refuses to accept this role, dismissing both Job and Job's God. When Shmuel accuses him of having pride in his bitterness, Yakov retorts by hurling invectives at

God for his treatment of Job: "To win a lousy bet with the devil, he killed off all the servants and innocent children of Job." Then Yakov chides himself for becoming so angry, asserting that both Job and God are inventions of man. The only thing a man can trust is his own reason. Unlike Job, Yakov, ultimately, has only himself to rely on. He gains nourishment from the awareness that he is helping others, but he must suffer alone, and only alone can he gain the spiritual freedom he yearns.

Critics have found various weaknesses in *The Fixer*, although there is little agreement on this subject. Perhaps the most telling criticism is that the novel suffers aesthetically from a forced emphasis on content and meaning, at the expense of character. The only fully developed character is Yakov. The others are often one-dimensional foils for him. This is especially true of the antagonists, none of whom is convincingly drawn. Grubeshov, for example, is presented as both a fanatical anti-Semite who persecutes Yakov even to the detriment of his career *and* as a political opportunist. This seeming contradiction might have been resolved had Malamud emphasized more the nature of anti-Semitism in Russia. In other words, providing more insight into the history and dynamics of anti-Semitism could have allowed Malamud to turn anti-Semitism into an expansive metaphor like Jewishness, thus providing a more proportionate balance of meaning and character.

This criticism is a valid one. A better understanding of the motives of Yakov's oppressors might, however, cause his whole incredible experience to seem more comprehensible and thus reduce the novel's overwhelming sense of existential terror.

According to Malamud's own account of the novel's origin, he was looking for a way of depicting injustice in America. He also wanted to suggest the suffering of the Jews under Hitler. As his conception took more specific shape, he incorporated details from what he considered to be other famous cases of injustice: Sacco and Vanzetti in America and Dreyfus in France. Finally the Beiliss case, a story he had heard from his father as a boy, became central. In the end, according to Malamud, "a novel that began as an idea concerned with injustice in America today has become one set in Russia fifty years ago, dealing with anti-Semitism there. Injustice is injustice."[2] In many ways, then, the Russia of Yakov Bok, like Sy Levin's Cascadia, becomes a metaphor for contemporary America. At the same time, *The Fixer* expresses existential suffering common to all people in the twentieth century.

Malamud's goal for *The Fixer* was ambitious; he wanted to produce a work of social relevance, but at the same time he sought to lift a discussion of important issues to the imaginative level of art. He succeeds in achieving this goal, for *The Fixer* clearly exemplifies Malamud's story-telling craftsmanship while it explores the human suffering caused by injustice and charts the spiritual growth and freedom that can transcend this suffering.

# 6

●●●●●●●●●●●●●●●●●●●●●●●●●●●●●●●●●●●●●●●●●●●●●●●●●●●●●●●●●●

# The Artist as Schlemiel:
# *Pictures of Fidelman:*
# *An Exhibition*

*Pictures of Fidelman* contains five previously published stories and one new story, all featuring as their
protagonist Arthur Fidelman. Malamud has done
more than simply collect the Fidelman short stories;
the stories show a development of character and structure close to that of a novel. The author has revealed in
more than one interview that his intention was to
develop one theme in the form of a picaresque novel
(that is, a novel presenting the episodic, comic adventures of a wily rogue as he comes into contact—often
on a journey or quest—with a wide cross section of
society). The work also bears a resemblance to the
*Bildungsroman*, a type of novel of character that deals
with apprenticeship or education. Both the picaresque
and the *Bildungsroman* lend themselves to the journey
motif that helps bind the Fidelman stories together.
The arrangement of the stories is careful and deliber-
ate, each one presenting an image of Arthur Fidelman.
The work as a whole is like an exhibition of pictures,
together forming a collage.

   The first picture of Fidelman, "Last Mohican,"
finds him, "a self-confessed failure as a painter," arriv-
ing in Rome to prepare a critical study of the Renais-
sance painter Giotto. The reader soon realizes that
Fidelman's change of residence has other causes. Like
Frank Alpine, Sy Levin, and Yakov Bok, Fidelman's

journey represents a search for a meaningful life. His search continues literally and figuratively as Fidelman wanders from town to town in Italy, from story to story in the book.

Upon his arrival in Rome, Fidelman is met by a Jewish refugee, a schnorrer (artful beggar), Shimon Susskind. Like Fidelman, Susskind is a Jew in a Christian land, making his living peddling whatever he can lay hands on, especially religious souvenirs for tourists. Unlike Fidelman, though, Susskind's knowledge of human nature allows him to manipulate people; Fidelman becomes one of his victims. When the American refuses to give the schnorrer his "old" suit of clothes (if one suit is new, the other must be old, Susskind reasons), Susskind steals the art critic's brief-case containing the first chapter of his book on Giotto. Fidelman is grieved over the loss because he at last "had mastered the problems of order and form."

Unable to continue without the missing chapter, Fidelman tries desperately to locate Susskind in hopes of recovering his work. He combs the Jewish ghetto, synagogues, tourist spots, "wherever people peddled," even the graveyard where, he has learned, Susskind sometimes "accepts" a small fee for reciting prayers for the dead; finally Fidelman finds the refugee selling rosaries outside St. Peter's cathedral. Quickly arranging a barter (suit in exchange for briefcase), Fidelman is agonized to discover that his "fine critical chapter" is not in the briefcase. Now the beggar turns critic as he explains that as a favor to Fidelman he has burned the chapter because "the words were there but the spirit was missing." Overcome by a murderous rage, Fidelman futilely chases the startlingly lightfooted schnorrer until suddenly, inspired by a vision of Giotto's painting of St. Francis giving his cloak to a beggar and "moved by all he had lately learned," he has a sudden insight. "Susskind, come back. . . . All is forgiven."

This first story, although somewhat self-contained, sketches the outline for the complete portrait. Fidelman talks to himself, finds (or places) himself in ludicrous situations, agonizes over the discrepancy between his high artistic aspirations and his lowly behavior, and always hopes for the best but expects the worst. The humor stems largely from the contrast within Fidelman's farcical adventures and his sublime aspirations, between his schlemiel behavior and his artistic pretensions.

Susskind's claim that he has done Fidelman a favor by destroying his manuscript raises the central question of the relationship of the artist's life to his work. The accuracy of Susskind's criticism—that Fidelman does not understand the spirit of Giotto— was previously suggested in Fidelman's dream-vision of Giotto's painting of St. Francis. Only after experiencing, for the first time, the master's compassion for humanity can Fidelman feel compassion for Susskind. The role of schnorrer as a representative figure of suffering humanity is made explicit in an exchange that continues to haunt Fidelman throughout the chronicle.* Susskind insists that Fidelman must be responsible for the schnorrer's fate. Why? asks Fidelman. "Because you are a man. Because you are a Jew, aren't you?" Susskind becomes for Fidelman a sort of dybbuk (demon) who inhabits his conscience, destroying his peace of mind.

As a "conscience figure," Susskind forces Fidelman to confront himself, to discover his own identity. In going to Italy Fidelman has rejected his family and his past. Like the "innocent abroad" characters of Henry James, Fidelman gets caught up in the glamor

---

*Because *Pictures of Fidelman* is more than an ordinary collection of short stories and yet lacks the plot unity of a novel, the term "chronicle" is used here to suggest something of the collection's continuity of episodes.

and romance of the Eternal City, but Susskind stops
the poor Bronx Jew from losing himself in the ecstasy
of an overexcited imagination. As Fidelman becomes
the pursuer rather than the pursued, he tracks Susskind through the Jewish ghetto with its narrow streets
full of bearded old Jews and echoing the muffled
sounds of Hebraic chants, past little synagogues, to the
Jewish cemetery where he reads tombstones recalling
the horrors of the Nazi holocaust. As calculating
dybbuk, Susskind demonically ushers Fidelman on a
guided tour of their ethnic heritage; Fidelman
necessarily takes inventory of his spirit and comes, par-
tially, to terms with himself.

In "Still Life," the second "picture," Fidelman
has abandoned the role of critic and has renewed his
prior attempt to become a painter. Answering an
advertisement to share a studio with another painter,
Fidelman finds himself falling helplessly in love with
the arty-looking woman, Annamaria, who answers the
door. "Fidelman loudly protested within—cried out
severely against the weak self, called himself ferocious
names," but all in vain as he ends up agreeing to pay
twice the advertised rate, paying cash "through both
nostrils" for the first and last months in advance, plus
a security deposit. He's hooked.

The artistic inadequacy that Susskind recognized
now becomes clear as the "art student," as he is now
called, proves incapable of painting anything original.
In his mind he fills his canvases with "harlequins,
whores, tragic kings, fragmented musicians, the sick
and the dead." These figures represent the reality of
what Fidelman feels inside, but he is so caught up in a
romantic view of art that what he actually attempts, a
traditional Mother and Child, quickly turns into a
Virgin and Child with his studio mate, Annamaria, as
the secret model. As a slave of love, he is reduced to
acting as Annamaria's janitor and lackey; as a painter

he can only imitate her poorly done work. She hides camouflaged crosses in her works to give them religious meaning; Fidelman lamely sneaks the Star of David into his paintings.

Annamaria is a delightful caricature of the self-absorbed, eccentric artist. She represents Fidelman's misguided notions about the artistic life. His only successful paintings are self-portraits that dredge up hidden needs and guilts, but his idealized view of art at first causes him to keep his real-life experience imprisoned in his imagination.

Fidelman learns little about art in this story, but enjoys a hilariously unexpected sexual victory over his eccentric companion. Not realizing that she is a superstitious religious fanatic who is guilt-ridden over once having drowned her bastard child, Fidelman decides to paint a "Portrait of the Artist as Priest" (an imitation of Rembrandt). Dressed in a rented cassock, Fidelman is more than a little surprised when Annamaria begs him for absolution, penance, and expiation through sexual intercourse. Fidelman is eager to oblige. "Pumping slowly he nailed her to her cross."

In "Still Life," Malamud plays off Fidelman's wild sexual encounters against his increasingly futile and desperate attempts to become an artist. This juxtaposition of the coarsely sexual with the sublimely aesthetic produces a kind of farcical humor that nonetheless continues Malamud's inquiry into the nature of art and the artist. In presenting an "exhibition of the artist as schlemiel," Malamud creates a humorous but probing exploration into the philosophy of art.

Picture number three, "Naked Nude," finds Fidelman in Milan, a homeless ex-artist turned pickpocket who has been blackmailed by two hoodlums (Angelo and Scarpio) into slaving away at menial labor in a brothel. When the gangsters learn that their captive was once an artist, they concoct a scheme to steal a painting by Titian ("Venus of Urbino") and replace it with a Fidelman forgery. To Fidelman's objections against the dishonesty of "stealing another painter's ideas and work," the brothel keeper assures him that Titian would not blame him, since he himself had modeled the figure of the Urbino on Giorgione's Venus. "Art steals and so does everybody. . . . It's the way of the world." Still unconvinced, Fidelman reluctantly agrees to cooperate when promised his freedom in return for a good likeness. This proves difficult for "the copyist," as he is now called, until he personally views the original painting and falls madly in love with Titian's Venus, whereupon he quickly completes the copy in a frenzy of passionate activity. On the night of the robbery, Fidelman is able to trick the thieves, make off with the Venus, and head for freedom. In a brilliantly ironic ending, Malamud reveals that Fidelman has chosen to steal his own reproduction of the Venus.

"Naked Nude" gives the reader insight into an unromanticized view of art: by having Fidelman steal his own imitation of Titian's Venus of Urbino, Malamud slyly suggests that the artist's passion for his work in reality contains more of narcissism than love of beauty. Fidelman, however, does not grasp this insight.

In picture four, "Pimp's Revenge," Fidelman now lives in Florence, where he sculpts Madonnas for tourists and sells his figures for a pittance to enable him to paint his masterpiece, "Mother and Son," the inspiration for which he takes from an old photograph of his mother and himself as a child. One day on his way to the market Fidelman meets a young prostitute named Esmeralda. She comes to live with him, mainly to escape her pimp, Ludovico, and becomes a virtual servant in Fidelman's shabby apartment. Esmeralda

later reveals that she went to live with Fidelman
because she thought an artist must know about life. All
she learns is that he is "like everybody else, shivering in
[his] drawers." Eventually Fidelman sends Esmeralda
back to work as a prostitute, promising to marry her as
soon as he finishes his painting. He even becomes her
pimp.

Explaining to Esmeralda why he is obsessed with
painting a picture of his mother, Fidelman says he
feels that if he can paint this picture, then somehow
the pieces of his life will fall into place. Each day he
works to capture the face of his mother, only to scrape
it all off at night in dissatisfaction. In the presence of
Esmeralda, however, he somehow begins to come to
grips with his elusive artistic vision.

Fidelman's psychological block is finally removed
after Esmeralda tells him that the figures in the painting give her the feeling that the son (Fidelman himself
as a boy) wants to be in his mother's arms. For a moment Fidelman is able to face the reality that he is a
pimp, a failure not worthy of appearing in the painting with his mother. Using Esmeralda as his model, he
abandons the "Mother and Son" and paints instead the
"Prostitute and Procurer." The portrait is indeed a
masterpiece of sorts, strong and convincing. However,
Fidelman's success is short-lived. Following the
deliberately bad advice of Ludovico, he retouches his
masterpiece, trying to make it "truer to life." After a
few quick brushstrokes, Fidelman, "sickened to his
gut," realizes he has ruined it.

"Pimp's Revenge" draws together most of the
themes of the collection. Fidelman shows how little he
understands the spirit behind various artistic move-
ments when he complains to himself that "everything's
been done or is otherwise out of style—cubism, sur-
realism, action painting. If only I could guess what's
next." Later in the story, Ludovico, the pimp turned

self-styled art critic, tells Fidelman ironically that there is nothing wrong with imitating the masters: "Thus new masters are born." By this time it is clear that, as Susskind had said, Fidelman's concern with artistic structure negates his becoming more than a devotee or a "copyist."

A related, but broader, theme—the inseparability of art and life—finds its focal point in this story. Asked by Ludovico whether he is a moral man, Fidelman seriously replies, "In my art I am." Later he tells Esmeralda that art is something different from life, something special without which he cannot exist. "If I'm not an artist, then I'm nothing." "My God," says Esmeralda, "aren't you a man?" "Not really, without art." In a long interview that becomes, in effect, a hilarious parody of a Socratic dialogue, Ludovico (one of a series of low-life characters turned art critic) demonstrates the illogic of statement after statement Fidelman makes about the special morality of art, leading the painter finally to a truth—that the morality of art and the morality of life are inseparable. Fidelman, however, is unable to accept this conclusion, preferring instead to view art as something sacred, entirely separate from the petty concerns of life.

Malamud treats the theme of the inseparability of the artist's life and his work—a counterpart of the theme of the inseparability of form and content—most thoroughly in relation to Fidelman's inability to complete his masterpiece. The truth is, Fidelman realizes, that painting is threatening to his artistic ego; it might lead to a painful self-discovery.

The fifth story, "Pictures of the Artist," takes Fidelman through the underworld of his own subconscious. In one dream sequence, we are told about the myth of Fidelman's death, which sounds suspiciously like an elaborate Jewish joke. It is said that the copyist ended his days exhibiting holes in the ground, explaining his creations with a pseudoaesthetic pitch about form being the content of art. After his last showing, Fidelman is visited by the cloaked figure of Death, who, like Susskind, accuses the sculptor-of-holes of not knowing "the difference between something and nothing." To illumine his criticism, the figure hits Fidelman over the head with a shovel and buries him in one of his own holes, exclaiming that now it is a grave: "We got form, but we also got content."

In another dreamlike sequence, Susskind appears as Christ preaching from a mountaintop, advising Fidelman to abandon his painting and become a disciple. Fidelman, however, acts the part of Judas, spending his traitor's reward on paints, brushes, and canvas. In a final imaginary sequence, a voice from a light bulb, sounding very much like Susskind, urges Fidelman to abandon his obsessive Michelangelo-like painting on the walls of a subterranean cave and go upstairs to say hello to his sister Bessie, whom he has not seen for years. Instructing the bulb to "Be my Virgil," Fidelman mounts the stairs and greets his sister on her death bed.

In "Pictures of the Artist," Malamud displays his innovative style and literary range: rapid shifts in setting, point-of-view, and diction produce a stylistic tour de force, a "neo-Joycean, comitragic, surrealistic, stream-of-consciousness, visionary sequence," as one critic has aptly described it.[1] For example: "Oil on wood. Bottle fucking guitar? Bull impaled on pole? One-eyed carp stuffed in staring green bottle? Clown spooning dog dung out of sawdust? Staircase ascending a nude?" Such disconnected, distorted allusions to masterpieces of modern art effectively express Fidelman's moral descent into the nightmare world of the artist's hell. After plumbing the black depths of madness, folly, evil, and despair, Fidelman begins his moral ascent. When he tells the light bulb, in the final section, to "Be my Virgil," he is acknowledging his acceptance of Susskind's spiritual guidance and expressing his desire to be led, like Dante, out of the pit of hell. His willingness to perform even a token act of kindness for his dying sister signals the beginning of his eventual insight into himself and into life.

"Glass Blower of Venice," a story written especially for the ending of *Pictures of Fidelman*, finds Fidelman in Venice, where he earns a meager living by ferrying passengers across the Grand Canal piggy-back style. One day Fidelman meets and seduces an Italian woman, Margheretta. As the affair continues, he becomes best friends with, and later lover of, her husband, Beppo, a glass blower who is very "wise about life." Beppo destroys all of Fidelman's old paintings because they are so bad, advising him not to waste his life creating bad art. Instead he should "invent life." Beppo instructs Fidelman in the craft of glass-blowing and teaches him how to love, something Fidelman does for the first time in his life.

The relationship is short-lived, however; Margheretta begs the "ex-painter" to leave Italy and allow Beppo to return to his family. Now capable of self-sacrifice out of love, Fidelman gives Beppo back to his wife. In the last lines of the story we are told that "Fidelman sailed from Venice on a Portuguese freighter," and that "in America he worked as a crafts-man and loved men and women."

Broadly speaking, the subject of *Pictures of Fidelman* is art. The chronicle raises such questions as art's role in life, the nature of good art (is it primarily a matter of talent or of vision, that is, character?), and the mysterious process by which the artist's experience in life, his suffering, becomes transformed into art. Malamud himself has stated that his goal was to have his comic hero "find himself both in art and self-knowledge.":[2] The chronicle of Fidelman is, in effect, a parable of the artistic and moral pursuit.

Fidelman's self-discovery is begun but by no means completed in the first story. As his comic adventures continue, Fidelman has layer after layer of superficial identity stripped away; episode by episode he slowly discovers a new dimension of identity as craftsman and lover. He learns to invent life as he ceases to imitate what he thinks is art. The reader realizes early in the chronicle that Susskind is really Fidelman's alter ego, representing a part of himself he would like to ignore. Fidelman is, then, symbolically pitted against himself. In the final episode of the last story, as in the opening one, we see that the acceptance of Fidelman's hidden self requires an expression of mercy, love, charity, or forgiveness to confirm his faith in himself and humanity.

In the last story, Fidelman completes his journey of moral self-discovery. The sometime critic, fool, forger, pimp, huckster, and Judas is saved by abandoning the pretenses of art for the honesty of craftsmanship and by giving life rather than taking it. Clearly, as many critics have suggested, Fidelman's willingness to accept and give love, even with the homosexual glass blower of Venice, signifies his acceptance of his past failures in life and art. However, the end of the story turns on an ironic ambiguity characteristic of Malamud. Could it be that like Columbus, an earlier explorer from Venice sailing on a Portuguese ship, Fidelman will mistake the New World for the Old?

In *Pictures of Fidelman* Malamud examines longheld views about the artist—that artistic vision is something of a sacred revelation, that artistic integrity is its own reward, that creative genius cannot be bound by conventional standards of morality. By presenting the artist as a schlemiel character whose

comic adventures, internal struggles, and moral com-
promises all go for naught artistically, Malamud
challenges these myths, forcing us to view them from a
new perspective. Fidelman does not end up like a Van
Gogh, whose eccentricities and human failings are
eventually forgiven because of his genius; rather, he
ends as he began, a failed artist, though perhaps a better human being. In a sense, Malamud's purpose is to
glorify art by ridiculing its excesses. In spite of expos-
ing clichés about art and parodying its pretensions,
Malamud really believes in art's sanctity. So authen-
tically does he capture the life and concerns of the artist that *Pictures of Fidelman* is sometimes used as a text
in college courses exploring the nature of modern art.

*Fidelman* is Malamud's most accomplished comic
work, as well as his most versatile and innovative
stylistic undertaking. Effectively using elements of
farce, parable, and the picaresque, Malamud creates a
folktale sense of fantasy that ought not be considered
naturalistically. For example, the idea of Fidelman
ferrying passengers across the Grand Canal on his
back, although presented matter-of-factly, is realisti-
cally absurd. It is as if Malamud invites the reader to
join him in enjoying the truth-in-fantasy inventiveness
of these folklike tales. Yet his attempt to create a
loosely structured picaresque novel is not entirely successful. Although Malamud, on his own testimony,
had the overall plan in mind from the beginning,
and although he carefully reworked the previously
published Fidelman stories, he did not succeed in
creating a unified whole. The final product seems as
much a collection of self-contained stories as a fully
unified novel.

More significantly, the book is uneven in quality
and texture. The first story, "Last Mohican," is as fine
a piece of writing as Malamud ever produced, but the
remainder of the book fails to sustain the brilliant

comic intensity of Fidelman's confrontation with his dybbuk, Susskind. Although Susskind's presence is occasionally felt lurking at the edge of Fidelman's consciousness during the rest of the book, some of the twisted, obsessive intensity of Fidelman's character is lost.

It is as if Susskind's physical presence is necessary to focus and dramatize for the reader the deeply self-combative nature of Fidelman's internal conflict. Or, to put the matter more simply, one might say that the characterization of Susskind in "Last Mohican" is as important to the reader as is the characterization of Fidelman. When Susskind later fades into the background as a shadowy figure who haunts Fidelman's subconscious, some of the substance of the reader's interest also disappears. Although other characters, such as the pimp, Ludovico, and Beppo, the glass blower of Venice, in turn provide a narrative focus in later episodes, only Susskind's interaction with Fidelman captures a sense of a primal—obsessive reciprocal, irrational and mysterious, though ultimately beneficial—bond of intimacy. After finishing the book, one's most powerful memory is of Fidelman and Susskind pursuing each other incessantly down the dark streets of their collective unconscious.

# 7

••••••••••••••••••••••••••••••••••••••••••••••••••••••••

# Mankind's Divided Self:
## *The Tenants*

In *The Tenants* Malamud returns to his familiar ter-
rain of gloomy, wasted, New York streets. The setting
of the story is an abandoned apartment house on East
Thirty-First Street which reeks of human excrement,
garbage, and dead rats. Harry Lesser is its sole tenant,
holding out against a landlord, Levenspiel, who wants
to tear down the rent-controlled building and realize
his dream of owning a row of shops under five floors of
apartments—to "make myself a comfortable life."
Harry, a Jewish writer in the tenth year of a struggle to
finish his third novel, refuses to leave the place of his
novel's birth until he can overcome a writer's block
and finally bring his creation to its conclusion. "Have
a little mercy, Lesser," pleads the landlord with his
statutory tenant, "move out so I can break up this rotten house that weighs like a hunch on my back." But
Harry's only concern is to finish his book. Even
Levenspiel's offers of increasingly larger sums of
money if Harry will leave the building fail. By the end
of the book Harry refuses $10,000 and remains bar-
ricaded behind the securely locked door of his flat.

The isolation of Harry's creative anguish is broken
one day when he discovers a squatter, a self-taught
black writer, Willie Spearmint, typing away in an ad-
jacent apartment. Approaching each other warily, the
two enter into a begrudging friendship. For a time, the
two men "embrace like brothers."

Harry Lesser's novel is about love, but he has so

isolated himself from others that he knows little of
love. He is a loner, locked in a prison of his own making. As his name implies, Lesser is far from perfect,
both as artist and as man. He has written one good
novel and one bad. Dedicated totally to his craft, he
now struggles with a third, ironically entitled *The
Promised End*, for which, because it parallels his own
life, he can find no ending. He is convinced that if he
can only work out an ending, he can discover what
love is. He thinks to himself, "Lesser writes the book
and the book writes Lesser." Harry exalts his role as artist, claiming that writing is his life. "He lives to write,
he writes to live." "For Christ's sake," Levenspiel
pleads, "what are you writing, the Holy Bible?" "Who
can say?" comes the self-satisfied reply. At the same
time, Harry fails to see that his obsession with art
prevents him from experiencing life.

Willie Spearmint is a self-taught, would-be writer,
who relies on his blackness and shattering ghetto
background to give shape to his fiction. Lacking any
sense of form or structure, he creates a sprawling, tortured, angry narrative as he tries to give expression to
the black experience. At the same time he tries to
throw off his tormented past through writing. Every
bit as obsessed with his writing as Lesser is with his,
Spearmint is torn between being artist or activist. His
conflict intensifies after he asks Lesser, as an experienced writer, to teach him about form: "if . . . I have
to learn something from whitey to do it better as a
black man, then I will *for that purpose only*."

Some time later Willie invites Harry to join an
impromptu party at the apartment of a black friend,
Mary Kettlesmith. During the evening Harry and the
hostess slip off to enjoy each other in bed. When Harry
rejoins the party afterward, he is faced by "a crowd of
silent blacks" and knows that his liaison has not gone
unnoticed. In an agonizing scene Harry undergoes an

ordeal by insult from Willie and his friends. As the racial ferocity of the insults escalates, Harry fearfully leaves the apartment, half expecting to be waylaid and beaten up before he reaches the street. The next day Willie explains that he led the verbal attack on Harry in order to prevent a more physical one. "That was how I saved your skin." The uneasy friendship continues.

The two writers become increasingly competitive as Harry tells Willie that in order to create art he must learn to control his anger and "make . . . outrage larger than protest." Willie shouts back, "I am art. Willie Spearmint, *black man*." Later he writes on the wall in large block letters: "Revolution is the real art." Their arguments about form and content, control and passion, art and revolution, become increasingly bitter. Willie struggles to learn the secrets of Harry's craft while at the same time trying to keep his mind from becoming polluted by Harry's "white" ideas.

Before long Harry begins an affair with Willie's Jewish girlfriend, Irene Bell (née Belinsky). After months of secret meetings with Irene, Harry finally tells Willie of their love and his intention to marry her. Willie retaliates by destroying Harry's manuscript; Harry smashes Willie's typewriter.

Rebounding from this disaster Harry tries desperately to reconstruct his novel, hoping this time to do a better job than in the previous draft. He becomes so obsessed by his writing that he begins seeing less and less of Irene. Then one morning he discovers in the rubbish can outside his building a "barrelful of crumpled yellow balls of paper." Willie has returned. Although he never catches a glimpse of his former friend, Harry each day reads Willie's discarded pages, keeping track, in this way, of the black man's tortured, angry struggle to become a writer. At night he prowls the deserted halls of the tenement searching for

Willie's lair. Lesser soon realizes that Willie is keeping track of Harry's progress in the same way.

In a climactic scene, more hallucinatory than real, the two writers meet in a dark hallway, transmuted by Lesser's fervid imagination into a primitive jungle, and lock themselves together in a bloody struggle: "Bloodsuckin Jew Niggerhater." "Anti-Semitic Ape." Acting out the last stage of their hatred for each other, Harry cleaves Willie's skull with an ax, while Willie castrates Harry with a razor-sharp saber. The final words of the novel are Levenspiel's, as he discovers the bodies and prays for mercy—for himself, for Lesser and Willie, and for mankind—"mercy, mercy, . . . mercy."

Progressively, in the course of the novel, Harry and Willie come to represent not only two writers— one a self-satisfied pedant enamored with form, the other an angry revolutionist striving to express black rage—but two racial identities representing two distinct cultural backgrounds. Dedicated to creating his own style and achieving high artistic standards, Harry finds Willie's lack of craft offensive. Thinking of himself almost totally as artist rather than Jew, Harry considers ethnicity an inadequate basis for art. Willie defines his writing as black writing—no white can understand it. "This is a *black* book we talkin about that you don't understand at all. White fiction ain't the same as *black*. It *can't* be."

As emblems, the Jewish writer represents a humanistic tradition that strives to advance civilization by using reason to discover the universal truths of human experience; the black writer is a symbol of a black community struggling to create a new black culture. He views the term "universal" as a weapon of the enemy. The two men also represent two aspects of Art. The white stands for responsible Form, the black for felt Experience. This openly symbolic nature of

*The Tenants* makes it, in effect, a parable of the black-white confrontation. It pits the notions of civilized white against savage black, love versus hate, reason versus instinct, Israel versus Ishmael.

More than this, however, the conflict symbolizes humankind's divided self. Willie's insistence that Harry criticize his book brings to the surface the conflict between Harry's two selves, causing his humanitarian instincts to vie with his self-centered absorption in writing. Harry, like Willie, is torn between his desire to be involved and his conviction that an aesthetic sense demands an alienating dedication. In this sense, Harry and Willie are mirror images of each other. Harry has struggled for a decade with a novel about a novelist writing a novel about a writer's deficiencies in compassion and love. Willie, similarly, tries to give shape to his rage by writing about a black writer's efforts to do the same. Harry lives his life through art; Willie struggles to give artistic shape to his life. Both fail to bridge the gap between art and life.

As mirror images of each other, the two writers need one another, repel each other, and suffer together. Harry's criticism of Willie's manuscript destroys the black's confidence in his writing; in stealing his girl, Harry undermines Willie's manhood. In Willie's view, Harry has castrated him and made him a victim. As the struggle intensifies, the two become locked in a twisted symbiotic relationship. They are aware of their work and each other—little else. (Irene disgustedly moves to San Francisco, leaving behind a farewell note saying she is more important than any book.) The symbolic landscape of ruined flats and smelly hallways is the only witness to their growing hatred.

Malamud's message is clear. Hatred breeds violence until the differences between victim and victimizer become blurred: they victimize each other. As Willie spews forth virulent anti-Semitic stories, Harry

becomes more and more despairing of ever being able
to finish his novel. Despite the high-minded invoca-
tions of art by the one and the revolutionary posturing
of the other, Harry and Willie both neglect the woman
they love. Both end by grubbing in the trash, looking
for each other's crumpled sheets of discarded writings,
and both end in savagery.

Malamud's narrative technique in *The Tenants*
moves his story away from realism towards fantasy.
Shifting from third-person to first-person perceptions,
and from narrative dialogue to reverie, all action is
filtered through Harry's thoughts and nightmares.
Malamud infuses even ostensibly "realistic" sections of
dialogue with an air of uncertainty by, for example,
occasionally omitting quotation marks and thus creating a feeling that the conversation may be interior. In
narrative passages, Malamud often uses a deliberately
choppy style, with many interruptions, that captures a
sense of Harry's disconnected thoughts, neurotic emotional life, and wild imagination, as in the following
passage:

On this cold winter morning when the rusty radiator knocked
like a hearty guest but gave off feeble warmth, yesterday's
snow standing seven stiff inches on the white street, through
which indigenous soot seeped, Harry Lesser, a serious man,
strapped his timepiece on his wrist—time also lived on his
back—and ran down six dirty flights of the all-but-
abandoned, year 1900, faded bulky brick tenement he lived
and wrote in.

The grim mood and realistic tenement setting slip
rapidly into a fact-and-fantasy world of imagination
that gracefully slides back and forth between delightful whimsy and unsettling savagery.

As Harry daydreams, a scene of a grafitti-jungle
mural in an empty apartment grows in his imagination
until Levenspiel's apartment house becomes trans-

formed into Harry's island-jungle-garden. In the
dreamscape, Willie and Harry begin life on the island
like brothers, artists together, floating down a jungle
river on a raft between crowds of people. Later a ship-
wrecked Harry is greeted by a voluptuous black girl.
In another hallucination, Willie appears as a cannibal
devouring the severed limb of a murdered white man.
By the end of the novel, the line between reality
and fantasy has become so blurred that Levenspiel's
building seems to have become entangled in thick
jungle foliage, "huge ferns, saw-toothed cactus taller
than men, putrefying omniverous plants"—a primeval
setting appropriate for the inevitable, savage confrontation between the two men.

In structure *The Tenants* is like a mirror. Spearmint and Lesser are mirror opposites of each other,
and both struggle to extract art from experience by
observing themselves living, writing, and coping with
the complex interplay of literature and life. This cir-
cularity, with all actions and implications turning
back upon themselves, gives a sense of images being
reflected in a mirror, the mirror images in turn being
reflected in another mirror, and so on. The effect is
like the old-fashioned barber shop experience of being
between two walls of mirrors: one looks at oneself
looking at oneself and seeing, seemingly, into infinity.
The refractive implications of *The Tenants* are conveyed through Lesser's thoughts, dreams, hallucinations, and nightmares. It is in these interior refractions
that the tension and violence build to a "final" scene
that spurts blood. But the reader suspects that neither
the blood nor the apocalyptic vision is real. Both are
likely the outpouring of Harry's overwrought imagination.

This ambiguity of refractive images of *The
Tenants* is reinforced by three dream-endings Harry
imagines for his novel. Early in the story he imagines

his novel dying in flames as Levenspiel burns down the building in a final desperate attempt to evict the uncooperative writer. "END OF NOVEL," writes Malamud, but when the narrative continues on a realistic level in the next chapter, the reader realizes that the fire was Harry's nightmare. The second dream-ending occurs near the conclusion of the novel. Harry imagines a double wedding on his island, now transformed into an African village. The village chief marries Harry and Mary Kettlesmith, the black woman Harry has rejected in favor of Willie's girl. The chief tells Harry to enjoy life and to bring his goals more in line with his capabilities. As part of the same ceremony a rabbi from America marries Willie and Irene. "Someday," the rabbi proclaims, "God will bring together Ishmael and Israel to live as one people. It won't be the first miracle." In answer to Irene's bewildered query about how this dream can be occurring, Harry replies, "It's something I imagined, like an act of love, the end of my book, if I dared." Unconvinced, even in a dream, Irene retorts, "You're not so smart." "THE END." But it is only a dream. The miracle that will bring Ishmael and Israel together can not happen in Malamud's book any more than it can happen in Lesser's.

The third dreamlike ending occurs as Harry and Willie act out their brutal surrealistic scene of double murder. Gone are the interracial miracles. Instead, the two men now stalk each other seeking revenge. Harry has one brief insight before his demise: "Each . . . feels the anguish of the other." The words "THE END" follow this dream-vision as they do the previous two, but the novel actually ends with Levenspiel's echoing cry for mercy and compassion.

This final fantasy of Harry's is sly. It is a sort of trick ending that allows both Harry and Malamud to "close" their novels. Earlier Harry laments that he is "missing something" in his search for a suitable ending for his novel. This "something," he decides, "begins in an end." In other words, he expects any ending he finds to become a beginning. Malamud's novel also has a circular plot and structure. *The Tenants* begins with Harry getting up in the morning and looking at himself in the mirror over his dresser. It ends with Harry's "final" moment of shared anguish—followed by Levenspiel's echoing cry. This ending allows Harry to release his own pent-up emotions. Having found what may be his elusive beginning-in-the-end, Harry, the reader suspects, will again awake to confront his reflection in the mirror above his dresser. Such are the ambiguities of the search for life and art and love. This ending also allows Malamud to voice his recurrent plea for mutual compassion and mercy. Levenspiel's cry is that of the innocent bystander. It underscores Malamud's conviction that no one escapes human involvements or needs.

Some reviewers have considered the ending of *The Tenants* a "cop-out," an attempt by Malamud to resolve literary tensions by using a "mirror trick." Even worse, these reviewers claim, is Malamud's heavy-handed use of racial stereotypes, especially the stereotypes that ascribe passion and instinct to blacks, reason and intellect to whites. Harry imagines Willie in the context of jungle rites and savagery; the black imagines the Jew as parasite and slumlord. As writers, Willie prides himself on his passion, Harry on his art. When they come to blows at the end of the novel, Lesser strikes at Willie's head, the seat of reason; Willie slashes at Lesser's genitals, the center of physical passion. Each, in other words, attributes to the other his own conception of himself.

Malamud has been taken to task especially for his portrayal of Willie. Some reviewers are dismayed, even angered, by a white liberal who has a black

writer pen such lines as, "If you was mine I would
blast you ass," and "I got nothin to be shame of."
Willie's writing is not only crude but unoriginal. Upon
first reading his work, Harry thinks that the same sort
of gut-level fiction has been written much better by
other black writers, such as Richard Wright and
Claude Brown. Later, the scraps of stories Harry picks
out of the garbage come to sound more and more like
the stereotyped media version of the rhetoric of black
hate. How, these critics ask, can we take such a cliché
seriously?

Willie Spearmint is undeniably a stereotype, a
sort of prefabricated black. Malamud shows his
awareness of the problem when he has Willie tell
Harry, "I hate all that shit when whites tell you about
black." Harry Lesser, however, is also a stereotype,
another version of the introverted, tortured Jewish intellectual. Willie, as stereotype, was created by the
literature and the politics of the black movement;
Harry derives from the stereotypic Jew created by such
post–World War II novelists as Saul Bellow, Philip
Roth, and Malamud himself. In treating his characters
as emblems of two different cultural traditions,
Malamud simply develops the symbolic overtones inherent in the stereotypes, but he manages to breathe
life into the stereotypes. Both Harry and Willie become real men, struggling to write real books. Willie's
anguish, as well as Harry's, is genuine and moving.
The masses of crumpled balls of typing paper that
Harry finds, the bits of stories and novels written and
rewritten, are the product of a convincing human
being.

Perhaps even more important, Malamud's mirror
structure of the novel, with its accompanying use of
dreamscapes that blur the line between fantasy and
reality, makes it difficult, in the end, to conclude that
one character is somehow "better" than the other.

Both are equally culpable. Malamud portrays Harry as
being personally selfish in his desire to create "universal" art, an obsession anything but rational. The irony
of this representative of humanistic tradition acting
inhumanely is underscored throughout the novel,
sometimes in small ways, sometimes emphatically.
Even before Willie appears on the scene Harry remains unmoved by the plight of a hungry, injured
stray dog that claws at his door one day. "Although it
made piteous noises, Harry grabbed the mutt . . . by
a frayed rope collar around the neck, and . . . succeeded in enticing him down the stairs and out of the
house." Later he initiates a secret liaison with his
friend's girl while continuing to offer literary advice.
Towards the end of the novel Harry tells Willie, in a
dream sequence, "I treated you like any other man."
In saying this, Harry intends to reaffirm his belief in
moral equality. The statement contains, however, an
additional meaning for the reader: "I treated you as
inhumanely as I treat all people."

Willie, on the other hand, who often seems to act
so irrationally, has a very reasonable and humanistic
desire to participate in creating a new black culture.
As the novel continues and the mirror images begin to
multiply—as fantasy and reality become increasingly
obscured—the distinction between the two characters
blurs. Willie's virulently anti-Semitic stories are mir-
rored by Harry's fantasies of primitive racial rites. Occasionally, even in Harry's dreams, the two exchange
identities, as when Harry marries Mary Kettlesmith
clad only in a loincloth while Willie marries Irene
dressed in a modern suit.

Near story's end Willie and Harry become the two
parts of one identity. Each is incomplete without the
other. After his typewriter is destroyed, Willie leaves
the tenement but finds himself forced, by some internal compulsion, to return. Only in the prison of

Levenspiel's building, face to face with his white counterpart—the two alone in a symbolic micro-cosm—can Willie feel whole, tortured though he is. And, in some strange way, Harry can only feel a connection with life when Willie is around to share his isolated struggle. Only together can Willie and Harry, black and white, face their mutual destiny. Through the ambiguity of the novel's ending, Malamud guides readers toward their own END OF NOVEL; he forces us to provide our own answer to the pressing twentieth-century question: how are we tenants of America and of Earth going to live together?

*The Tenants* succeeds as parable because of Malamud's imaginative and controlled use of fantasy to underscore the paradoxes and ambiguities of existence in the modern world. The novel is alive and vibrant with humor and insight. Writing at a time when racial riots were tearing apart the fabric of society, Malamud crafted a courageous personal statement about the plight of humankind in late-twentieth-century America. In form as well as subject, *The Tenants* is a very American novel. Like Hawthorne's *House of the Seven Gables* and Faulkner's *Light in August*, it is a romance-novel containing moral allegory and a violent climax. Malamud's success in creating this difficult and ambitious form of novel testifies to both his impressive literary skill and his deep moral commitment to the belief that compassion and understanding must, and can, prevail if civilization is not to be destroyed by crippling conflicts between and within all of us.

# 8

## A New Life Revisited:
## *Dubin's Lives*

In an interview held on the eve of publication of his most recent novel, *Dubin's Lives* (1979), Malamud explained that the new book represents his attempt at bigness, at summing up what he has learned during his life. It differs from his earlier works, he said, in that "the texture of it, the depth of it, the quality of human experience in it is greater than in my previous books."[1] *Dubin's Lives* is a long and ambitious novel about love, marriage, old age, and youth.

The central character, William Dubin, at fifty-six, is a professional biographer, whose books about Lincoln, Mark Twain, and Thoreau have won universal praise and a presidential medal. He and his wife of more than twenty-five years, Kitty, live in Center Campobello, a small town in upstate New York near the Vermont border. Every day he takes a long walk, observing nature, à la Thoreau. Kitty gardens and works part-time in the local library. Their two children are grown but unfulfilled. Gerald, Kitty's son by her brief first marriage, lives bitterly as a U.S. Army deserter in Stockholm, while their daughter, Maud, the apple of Dubin's eye, is studying at Berkeley and seldom communicates. When the novel opens in 1973, Dubin, after several years of research, is just beginning a biography of D. H. Lawrence.

Into the Dubin household comes a twenty-two-year-old college dropout and refugee from an upstate Buddhist commune, Fanny Bick, whom Kitty has

101

hired as a "cleaning person." Barefoot, bra-less,
dressed in a black shirt and wrap-around denim skirt,
Fanny radiates an air of sexual freedom even while
yanking the vacuum cleaner around the large, ram-
bling house. Though aroused by Fanny, Dubin maintains his self-control when she enters his study and
seductively unwraps her skirt. "Whatever it is you're
offering . . . I regret I can't accept." Fanny soon
leaves Center Campobello, but she has aroused in
Dubin his fiery but aging demon of lust. The rest of the
novel follows Dubin's on-again, off-again affair with
Fanny during two and a half years set against the
background of the changing seasons and the slow,
often blocked, evolution of Dubin's book on
Lawrence, the prophet of the natural life and of sexuality as "a dark force of blood consciousness."

The affair begins badly. Dubin arranges a rendezvous in New York City, but Fanny fails to show up.
Several weeks later Dubin whisks her off to Venice for
what he assumes will be a week of adulterous bliss, but
the trip turns into a humiliating fiasco. Through a
series of accidents their lovemaking is delayed again
and again. One day Dubin returns to their hotel room
two hours late to find Fanny making love with a hand-
some gondolier.

On his return home, clawed by guilt and frustration, Dubin sinks into a winter-long depression. His
marriage continues to deteriorate as he withdraws into
a self-imposed isolation; he cannot work, cannot sup-
press his irritation with Kitty's idiosyncrasies and
neuroses, and cannot get nubile Fanny out of his
mind. He tries to overcome his inertia with a rigorous
regimen of work, diet, and exercise, which fails to
stimulate his writing while torturing his middle-aged
flesh. In the spring, however, Fanny reappears in
Center Campobello, and they plunge into an ecstatic
affair that proves to be as salutary for his book on

Lawrence as it is for his masculine self-esteem. "These visits to Fanny sparked his work. Ideas swarmed into Dubin's mind."

Dubin continues to visit Fanny every few weeks in New York, and she occasionally sneaks into Center Campobello for a rendezvous. As the affair blossoms, Dubin experiences a great sensual awakening that unlocks a previously unexpressed part of his psyche and helps him to understand Lawrence. "His experience with Fanny, in variety, intensity, excitement heightened by her watchful curious knowing, sureness of her sexual self, willingness to give, couldn't have come at a better moment. He understood Lawrence more fully." But as Dubin becomes more involved in his work, he begins to neglect Fanny, seeing her less and less frequently.

Dubin now goes through another long depression, complicated by problems with his children, a growing desire for solitude, and increasing isolation from his wife, with whom he finally becomes impotent. However, Fanny returns, this time to settle in Center Campobello for good. She reawakens Dubin's sexuality, and an equilibrium of sorts is reached: Dubin goes to see Fanny on her neighboring farm several evenings a week while pretending to work on his biography. In the last sentences of the narrative Dubin leaves her house one night, runs past the waiting figure of her young local suitor, back to his wife "up the moonlit road, holding his half-stiffened phallus in his hand, for his wife with love." On the final page appears a bibliography of works by William B. Dubin, revealing that he does complete *The Passion of D. H. Lawrence: A Life*, and goes on to write two more books: *The Art of Biography* and *Anna Freud* (with Maud D. Perrera, apparently his estranged daughter).

To all outward appearances William Dubin is a settled, methodical man of habit, "a controlled type."

He has a solid literary reputation and thinks of himself
as a good if not daring writer. He fears "ineptitude,
imbalance, disorder" and "writes lives he can't live."
Through his biographies he feels he has learned how to
live life. "Those who write about life reflect about
life . . . you see in others who you are." Although occasionally adulterous during the last twelve of his
twenty-five years of marriage, Dubin considers
himself a settled family man. But after being aroused
by Fanny, Dubin's inner life bears little resemblance
to his outer one. Suddenly afraid that he has "missed
life," Dubin develops a Lawrence-like yearning for the
exuberance of the flesh, justifying it to himself as
something he deserves at his age. "I'm not twenty, nor
forty—I'm fifty-seven. Surely these years entitle me to
this pleasure."

Dubin's transformation is not as sudden as it
seems at first. From the beginning he has deep divi-
sions within his own being, as suggested by the pun in
the title. As a biographer Dubin is a thief of "lives"; he
has come to the craft by way of composing obituaries
for a New York newspaper: "In biographies the dead
become alive, or seem to." An "odd inward man," by
his own account, "held together by an ordered life,"
he has given up life to write lives, "a way of both
cultivating and resisting a powerful "inclination to a
confined lonely life." Yet at the same time Dubin is a
collector of lives, driven by a "hunger to live many
lives," so long as the one who lived the life is illustrious
and dead. When he is not writing lives, ransacking
them for their secrets, he is reading them, feverishly,
one after the other, a man "famished for lives" to com-
pensate for the quietness and isolation of his own. In
the lives of others he seeks to discover "how men hold
themselves together." Vigorous without, he is lan-
guishing within from unending introspection; almost
against his will, he profoundly yearns for a new life.

Dubin responds to Fanny with the whole of his repressed, buried being, exploding the bonds of his "ordered life," swept by his powerful feelings of yearning, loss, remorse, and jealousy. Feeling betrayed by Fanny even before they have become lovers, Dubin breaks down: his marriage, his work, his life, his very sanity become discomposed. When Fanny comes again into his life, Dubin's newly regained and hard-won sense of order quickly crumbles in the face of his yearning for a new life, but he enters into the affair wholeheartedly. However, this brings him a new problem. He is not a good liar and the secrecy of the affair further debilitates his marriage. "One may be able to mask dishonesty," he thinks, "but not its effects." After Fanny ends the romance, Dubin suffers from a psychologically more crippling conflict: his desire for the affair to be renewed wars with his self-hatred for ever having begun it. He is caught.

Kitty Dubin is an intelligent, complex, attractive woman of fifty, without vocation except as wife and mother. Self-analytic and unflinchingly honest, she also suffers from "the clinging remains of trauma" from her earlier life: her father committed suicide at thirty-four and her first husband died of leukemia at forty. An insomniac who worries about cancer and leaking stove-gas, Kitty mourns for her absent children and ruminates endlessly about her loving first husband. Her marriage to Dubin was, in a sense, arranged. As a young widow bringing up a son, Kitty had been torn between her fear of being hurt by another involvement and her need for warmth and affection. She wrote a self-advertisement for a newspaper, then changed her mind and withdrew it, but not before Dubin had seen it. He wrote to her; she replied; they were moved by each other's letters. They arranged a meeting, liked each other, and agreed to marry. "Strangers approaching each other," Dubin recalls, "in simple good faith: an act of trust was the imagined beginning." Now, twenty-five years later, Kitty clings to a dependent, tortured love for Dubin; she is a woman ready to respond warmly to affection but is hurt and resentful when it is withheld.

The same age as Dubin's daughter, Fanny Bick is alive, adrift in freedom. The product of an unhappy family background, she became independent at a young age. Her first lover, when she was still in high school, was a Jersey City orthodontist with a taste for kinky sex. During three years of college, Fanny concentrated more on sex than her studies, but dropped out and joined a Buddhist commune in an effort to make more of her life. Fanny wants what she wants, but on her own terms. Dubin finds himself alternately attracted to and repelled by her free-and-easy lifestyle. After discovering her with the gondolier in their hotel room in Venice, Dubin tries to dismiss her as a promiscuous juvenile, but later he comes to realize that she had acted in part out of resentment at the role he had forced upon her, that of attractive young companion of questionable morals whom he must keep at an emotional distance.

After Dubin begins visiting Fanny at her apartment in New York City, she seems changed; being with him gives her a feeling of self-mastery. He and his books lead her to want to make more sense of her own life. Indeed, late in the novel, we learn that Fanny had originally gone to Center Campobello out of a vague desire to meet Dubin: while at the commune she had read his biography of Mark Twain and decided that its author must know a lot about life. Hearing that he lives in a small town nearby, she goes there. Later, as she grows into womanhood, Fanny demands more direction and self-discipline in herself and more commitment from her lover. Her growing self-respect is emphasized when she feels humiliated after narrowly escaping discovery by Kitty Dubin. Later, Fanny breaks off the affair saying, "I'm not someone who's around just to keep your mind off old age. I have got to be more to you than a substitute for your lost youth, whatever the hell that is."

The themes of *Dubin's Lives* are many and complex. Central is the desire for a new life. At one point Dubin thinks, "Lives ought to begin again around fifty." On another occasion he tells himself, "One had to be daring before it was too late." Dubin's choice of Lawrence as a subject reveals his hunger for a new life. His wife, friends, and even his daughter all express bewilderment that he should choose to write about a man so totally different from himself. Dubin can only reply that he did not choose Lawrence; Lawrence, in a sense, chose him, as if he had something he wanted him to learn.

Near the beginning of the novel Dubin tells Fanny, "Be kind to yourself." At the end of the book, Fanny's last words to him are, "Don't kid yourself." The two imperatives define the double-edged nature of Dubin's search for a new life, a search bounded on one side by the yearning to experience the fullness of life in all its sensuality, vitality, and freedom; on the other by self-deception. Dubin is good at kidding himself. He ends up treating both his wife and his mistress badly—he will not leave Kitty for Fanny but neither will he give up Fanny. He can see that Kitty senses his withdrawal from their marriage, sees her becoming more and more lonely, but continues dreaming about a new life with Fanny, to whom he nonetheless will not make a full emotional commitment.

Dubin does, however, learn something from the suffering of his dilemma. At the beginning of the novel he knows that "all biography is ultimately fiction" but thinks that "the thousands of lives I've read and the

few I've written . . . [will] make the difference between badly and decently knowing." By the end he
knows "life is forever fleeting, our fates juggled heart-
breakingly by events we can't foresee or control and
we are always pitifully vulnerable to what happens
next."

Related to his search for a new life is the conflict
between life and work. Early in the novel, Kitty asks
her husband, "When will you take time to live?" The
biographer replies, "Writing is a mode of being. If I
write I live." When his work is going badly, Dubin
feels half-dead and moves about like a zombie, brood-
ing over his stalled book. When it is going well, he
feels alive and vibrant, but becomes so immersed in his
writing that he neglects both Kitty and Fanny. By the
novel's end, however, Dubin no longer "writes lives he
can't live." He has learned that "language is not life"
and that he had nearly "given up life to write lives."

The corollary to Dubin's search for a new life is
his fear of aging. "My concern with aging," he tells
himself near the end of the novel, "has made me
conscious of death." He had "entered the age of
aging. . . . He feared illness, immobility, the disgrace
of death." He had come to fear time as the ally of
death, "Time preached dying." In effect, Dubin feels
torn between two different conceptions of time and
old age: they are supposed to bring wisdom and dignity, but they also bring death. One aspect of time, the
past, is represented by Kitty. She is continually thinking of her first husband, yearning for her grown-up
children, analyzing the long years of her second marriage. Fanny, on the other hand, represents the future.
Dubin's dilemma is how to balance the commitments
of the past against the potential of the future as he attempts to find a new life in old age.

After his humiliating fiasco in Venice, Dubin
likens himself to "a broken clock—works, time, man-

gled. What is life trying to teach me?" The answer he
receives can be phrased as a riddle: life is trying to
teach what life teaches—life. The ambiguity of this
answer is underscored by the equilibrium reached at
the end: Dubin is unwilling to give up either Fanny or
Kitty. We never learn the outcome of this conflict, but
it is irrelevant, for the real story has already been told.
The point is that such knowledge as time grants has
been attained; Dubin's "lives" are now essentially one.
Readers must learn their own lessons.

Central to both Dubin's search for a new life and
his need to reconcile the conflicting demands of life
and work is his struggle to write a biography of D. H.
Lawrence. In his hunger for the renewal of spirit and
temporary redemption from the fact of aging that
Fanny affords him, Dubin finds himself embattled
with his book. At the heart of Dubin's condition is a
Lawrencian yearning of the flesh, for its wisdom and
power. But Lawrence was a man who wove myths
around himself: the prophet of sexual freedom was
embroiled in an "eternal domesticity" with his wife,
impotent at forty-two, enormously complicated, and,
in certain profound respects, inaccessible. In struggling to come to terms with Lawrence, Dubin endeav-
ors to understand himself. That he completes his biography of Lawrence suggests that he also succeeds in
resolving his own internal conflicts.

Structurally, Malamud uses D. H. Lawrence as a
framework that influences every aspect of the novel,
giving insight into Dubin's character, deepening the
themes, shaping the narrative. In terms of character,
Malamud makes the reader aware of many parallels
between the biographer and his subject, despite the
surface differences. Like Lawrence, Dubin has soaked
himself in nature, reveling in the names of flowers.
And Lawrence, like Dubin, was a closet prig who suffered from impotence. Dubin learns from Lawrence,

and, in the process, the reader gains insight into Dubin. Dubin often thinks about Lawrence, reads about him, and quotes him as he struggles to come to terms with the Lawrence in himself. "How curious it is, Dubin thought, as you write a man's life, how often his experiences become yours to live. This goes from book to book: their lives evoke mine or why do I write? I write to know the next room of my fate. To know it I must complete Lawrence's life." Elsewhere Dubin thinks, "I must stop running from Lawrence's dying. I must act my age."

Thematically, Malamud, through Dubin, uses Lawrence as a source of commentary on such things as marriage, women, love, sex, nature, and the art of biography. In addition, Malamud builds into the structure of his novel Lawrence's sense of the cycle of the seasons as an embodiment of the never-ending process of death and resurrection. Dubin, like Lawrence, sets his internal clock by the changing seasons. Two whole years undergo the cycle of efflorescence, decay, death, and rebirth. Dubin fights winter "as if it were the true enemy." Dreading its arrival, he thinks of August as "a masked month: it looked like summer and conspired with fall; like February it would attempt to hide what it was about." He revels in spring when it finally comes, gorges himself on summer, experiences both the glory and the threat of autumn. He feels himself aging, fears that he is losing his memory and his potency. But seasons of renewal occur; his work thrives, he feels rejuvenated in Fanny's arms.

Malamud keeps the reader constantly aware of the parallels between Dubin and Lawrence by building into the narrative echoes of Lawrence's life and works. During the first winter, for example, Dubin nearly dies when caught in a blizzard—an incident that seems to echo, distantly, the snowy death of

Gerald Crich in *Women in Love*. The explicit scenes of lovemaking also recall Lawrence. In one instance, Malamud makes a direct reference to the notorious scene between Connie Chatterley and her husband's gamekeeper, Mellors, in *Lady Chatterley's Lover*: as Lawrence's biographer lies in Fanny's bed, "Fanny, with her nail scissors, snipped the thorns off the rose and wound its green stem around his erect cock and kissed the white flower."

A less important but noticeable part of the structure of this novel lies in its symmetry. Pairs of incidents and characters contain obvious parallels. The narrative takes us through two complete cycles of the seasons—two winters of depression and internal suffering, two springs of hope and possibility, two summers of relative contentment, two autumns of uncertainty. Twice Dubin undergoes physical danger—first when he is lost in the blizzard, again a year later when a suspicious farmer mistakes him for a prowler and shoots at him. In the first instance he is rescued by his wife, the second time by his lover. Malamud provides many parallels between Fanny and Dubin's daughter Maud. Both drop out of college, both enter Buddhist communes, and both have affairs with men old enough to be their fathers. And, of course, Malamud establishes a parallel between Dubin and Lawrence, as well as an implied parallel between Maud and Anna Freud.

In unraveling his narrative Malamud uses a variety of techniques. Much of the novel is given over to Dubin's inner life as he analyzes all that happens around him. Hardly an event occurs without being filtered through his consciousness, subjected to his commentary. After first conversing with the new "cleaning person," for example, Dubin returns to his study, where he analyzes his response to the girl:

. . . it annoyed him a bit that he had felt her sexuality so

keenly. It rose from her bare feet. She thus projects herself?—
the feminine body—beautifully formed hefty hips, full bosom,
nipples visible—can one see less with two eyes? Or simply his
personal view of her?—male chauvinism: reacting reduc-
tively? What also ran through his mind was whether he had
responded to her as his usual self, or as one presently steeped
in Lawrence's sexual theories, odd as they were. . . . Dubin
counteracted the effect by recalling the continuous excitement of Thoreau, woodsy dybbuk, possessing him as he was
writing his life.

This passage is characteristic of the self-absorbed style
of Dubin's inner monologue as he endlessly analyzes
himself and his life. He is thus revealed as a man who
questions every shift in his mood or feelings, who tries
consciously to recall what he has learned from the lives
he has read and those he has written. One also hears in
Dubin's interior monologues echoes of his childhood in
a Jewish neighborhood of Newark, New Jersey. The
unexpected questions to himself ("She thus projects
herself?"), often coupled with a folksy expressiveness
("can one see less with two eyes?"), frequent interruptions, and occasional Yiddish words (dybbuk) give a
faint ethnic air that makes the voice of the interior
narrative peculiarly Dubin's.

Malamud also provides a more objective commentary on Dubin's behavior from the concealed narrator's point of view, although usually this external
voice blends into Dubin's own so easily that the two
are difficult to distinguish. For example, while on the
plane to Venice with Fanny, Dubin feels a momentary
pang of guilt. Then the narrator steps in and tells us,
"Dubin's difficulty was afterthought: he regretted
deceiving Kitty." Immediately Dubin's voice reasserts
itself, "There ought to be a better way. He recalled
Lawrence's remark: 'Honesty is more important than
marital fidelity.' " As if to emphasize Dubin's self-
preoccupation and sense of self-importance, the nar-

rator always refers to him as "Dubin" or "the biographer," while using only the first names of the other characters.

In the scenes that contain dialogue as well as narrative, Dubin's consciousness is also pervasive—his thoughts about what has been said are revealed every few lines. Most of the dialogue occurs either between Dubin and Kitty, endlessly discussing their marriage or their children, or between Dubin and Fanny, discussing their affair.

To keep the narrative moving, Malamud introduces rapid and unexpected shifts in subject or style. One section of the novel uses an especially striking device for conveying Dubin's thoughts, particularly the necessary background about Dubin and his wife. Malamud sets up an imaginary interview in which Dubin answers questions put to him by an imaginary interlocutor (who asks direct questions of the kind Kitty is partial to), the whole interspersed with short sections that continue the main thread of the narrative in the present. Another of these techniques to create surprise is the inclusion of little set pieces, containing a hint of fantasy, that are detached from but related to the main narrative:

On the road a jogger trotted toward him, a man with a blue band on his head.

    He slowed down as Dubin halted.

    "What are you running for?" the biographer asked him.

    "All I can stand to do. What about you?"

    "Broken heart, I think."

    They trotted in opposing directions.

Even more than narrative devices, it is Malamud's style that keeps the writing vital, continually altering in tone. Minute, imaginative observations of the changing New England landscape abound. We read, for example, that as spring approaches, "the melting snow uncovered meadows wet with grass in soggy clumps and swaths, as though the earth was strewn with soaking rags of brown, yellow, faded-green. After a long rain the bare tree trunks turned brown or black." Often the style is delightfully adventurous. After the Venice fiasco Dubin "returned heavier than he'd left, as though misery had paid interest in flesh." When Fanny and Dubin are in bed together Malamud writes, "They wrestled in her narrow bed, she with her youth; he with his wiles."

One element of the style can easily be overlooked: Malamud's mastery of the rhythms and nuances of Jewish expressiveness, here used so subtly that the reader often is charmed by the style without recognizing the Yiddish influence. When describing August as "a masked month" Malamud adds, "The leaves, if you touched, were drying." The interruption of the flow by the phrase "if you touched" and the omission of "them" after "touched" lends a Yiddish air to the sentence. A little further on Malamud writes, "He followed the flight of a crow elated to know who was flying." We are surprised to find "who" where we could expect "what." The result is a folksy we're-all-in-it-together stance, a sense of the equality of all Nature's creatures.

Unfortunately, as a large book *Dubin's Lives* creates for itself some large problems. Most obvious are the melodramatic plot twists. Will Dubin die in a blizzard? Will his wife discover Dubin and Fanny making love in the barn? What will happen to Dubin's expatriate son and his dropout daughter? On one occasion Dubin, in a fit of insomnia, wanders about a farmer's field in the middle of the night. He is attacked by a dog, chased up a tree, shot at, and—in a perfectly absurd coincidence—is picked up at 2:00 A.M. by Fanny, who has just returned from California to become owner of a nearby farm. Malamud appears to

introduce these melodramatic effects as an antidote to
the excessive length of his novel. The reader, like
Dubin, can only take so much of the weather, internal
suffering, and domestic bickering. Malamud makes his
points, then makes them again, and yet again.

Much of the melodrama concerns Dubin's son and
daughter. Near the end, as if aware of a need to liven
things up, Malamud introduces so many new com-
plications that the action becomes frenetic. Gerald, a
deserter from Vietnam, ends up as a reluctant Soviet
agent. Maud is "into mysticism" and becomes pregnant by a black man three times her age. These new
plot twists are so inadequately developed they become
absurd. They seem created simply to add to Dubin's
existential woes.

In addition, a number of the characterizations
are weak. Gerald and Maud remain unconvincing
background characters. Kitty nearly comes to life but
serves primarily as an antagonist for Dubin. Fanny, as
the maturing young woman of the later sections, has
less substance than Kitty. We are told that she sees
Dubin as lover, friend, and father, but the dynamics
of her personality remain too obscure for us to understand fully her need for a lover thirty years her senior.
A few words about an unsatisfactory father are not
enough. The parallels between Fanny and Maud fail
to convince and serve mostly to cause us to question
the characterization of each. Throughout, Fanny remains little more than a stereotype of the promiscuous
semi-hippie. She seems to speak every word of hip
slang Malamud can think of: "Her orgasm, she swore,
spaced her," or "I dig that," or "that's cool," or "he
flipped," or "don't sweat it, William," or "let's zap out
and see the sights." It is not so much that her speech is
off or inauthentic as that Malamud is unable to handle
it smoothly—a far cry from his sureness in handling
immigrant English.

An even more serious problem involves the presentation of Dubin himself. How ironically are we meant to perceive him? Or how sympathetically? In attempting to capture big truths—the wisdom of a lifetime—Malamud puts into Dubin's mouth sententious words of wisdom, often culled from the writings of dead literary figures: Montaigne, Samuel Johnson, Plato, Freud, Nietzsche, Robert Frost, T. S. Eliot, Thomas Hardy, William Wordsworth, St. Augustine, Chekhov, Thomas Carlyle, as well as Thoreau and Lawrence.

We cannot easily reconcile Dubin's sententious wisdom with his self-absorbed narrowness. For example, near the very end of the novel, Dubin sits up suddenly while in Fanny's bed to tell his lover:

To be honest . . . William Dubin, the biographer, is grateful to you for having through the years described to him what his lacking love, lacking nature, come to—for having kept him up with himself so that he could be a truthful measure, as well as recorder, of the lives of those he writes about, and therefore a better biographer.

Are Dubin's words those of wisdom or naiveté? Is this parody or Malamud during a weak moment? The reader simply does not know how to take it.

The problem is that no defining outline of the character has emerged. Malamud has positioned himself too close to Dubin to set him in perspective—either for Malamud or his reader. How, for instance, is the reader, psychologically and morally, to take Dubin's withdrawal from Kitty, his dalliance with Fanny? Is Dubin to be regarded as risking himself for a "plenitude of life through love?" As a middle-aged fool? Both? Malamud's characterization provides no answers.

Yet *Dubin's Lives* has many strengths. In addition to providing sensitive descriptions of nature, some exquisite set pieces, and frequent triumphs of style,

Malamud effectively immerses the reader in Dubin's struggles with his work and with his two long depressions. "As the days went by, the depression he had held off with upraised hands, as though it was a poisonous cloud, slipped through his fingers and smote him with suffocating force. It fell on his head like a smothering garment." The slow, steady, implacable, hour-by-hour dismantling of a disciplined life creates a powerful intensity of feeling. Dubin's fear of aging is also presented effectively. "A shocking multitude of single hairs appeared in his comb. A rotting tooth had to be pulled. He held a book two feet from his face to focus the words. His handwriting grew in size: he'd been avoiding glasses." One of the most moving sections in the novel occurs when Dubin fears that he is losing his memory, the writer's particular terror. "You had this thing to say and the words would not come. . . . Dubin, against the will, actively forgot names, details, words. He was losing them as though they were coins dropping out of holes in his pockets; or out of his raddled brain. They fell like raindrops into a stream—go find them."

The slow disintegration of Dubin's marriage provides the best-sustained writing in the novel. The reader is drawn into a domestic battleground, full of subterfuge, lies, deception, slights, injuries, indignities, small irritations absurdly magnified, unceasing quarrels about insignificant things that are really about everything that matters, the abrasions of a lifetime. William and Kitty Dubin are people of good will, a man and a woman eager to love each other; yet, on more than one occasion, "They faced each other in hatred." He cannot bear to hear her gargle. She cannot stand to hear him talk into his mirror. She buys him a newspaper; one of the pages is torn; he ostentiously mends it with tape.

Getting into bed that night after he had gone downstairs to

make sure he had locked the front door, as Dubin lay back his head cracked against hers. Kitty screamed. He bellowed: "How the hell did I know your head was on my pillow!"

"I wanted to be affectionate." Tears flowed from her eyes.

The image of Lawrence casts a curious shadow over *Dubin's Lives*. In the prepublication interview Malamud said that he wanted "Lawrence's theories [to] give the world of sex a kind of deepening." He had read only one or two books by Lawrence when he started *Dubin's Lives*, but since then had read everything. "If I ever knew a writer," he said, "I knew *him*. . . . I felt more respect for him after I got the feeling of the whole man."[2] Shades of William Dubin! One could ask of Malamud what is continually asked of his protagonist, "How can you hope to understand a writer so unlike yourself?" One gets the feeling that Malamud, like Dubin, is constitutionally unable to understand Lawrence. Yet both keep trying. And here, perhaps, is the key to understanding Malamud's successes and failures in *Dubin's Lives*. The real subject of the novel is a life battling with itself and the effects of time—the effects of aging, the loneliness and paralysis of a long marriage, the desire for a new life. The central relationship—the emotional center of the novel—is not between Dubin and Kitty, nor Dubin and Fanny, but between Dubin and Malamud. This is the source of both the power and the weakness of the novel; thus we see Malamud at his best and his worst. A kind of grim beauty emerges as Malamud tracks Dubin through his life, just as Dubin stalks Lawrence, dogging his steps, analyzing his every thought—in an unsuccessful attempt to find some way of resolving Dubin's conflicting needs and desires. At heart, *Dubin's Lives* is a parable of the writer's agonizing search for self-understanding.

# 9

## The Haunting of America: Malamud's Short Stories

During the past thirty years, Malamud has published more than forty stories, most of them collected in four volumes: *The Magic Barrel* (1958), *Idiots First* (1963), *Pictures of Fidelman: An Exhibition* (1969), and *Rembrandt's Hat* (1973). Malamud is a master of the short story. His first collection of stories, *The Magic Barrel*, winner of the National Book Award, is as well known and admired as any of his novels, and many of his stories have been widely anthologized.

The principal subject of Malamud's short stories is the ambivalence of human nature. "The Bill" (1951), for example, emphasizes the duality of human nature in which compassion wars with self-interest, conscience with greed. A tenement janitor, Willy Schlegel, takes advantage of a neighborly grocer, Mr. Panessa, by running up a bill of eighty-three dollars and then switching to a nearby self-service market. Obsessed by guilt, he develops a hatred for the elderly Panessa. When he receives a letter from Mrs. Panessa pleading for ten dollars for her sick husband, Willy hides in the cellar, but the next day he pawns his overcoat and runs back with the money—only to discover the grocer being carried off in a coffin. Willy's sinking heart becomes "a black painted window. . . . And the bill was never paid." The ending of the story makes clear to the reader that Willy has turned Mr. Panessa's gift into an emotional debt that he can never repay, although it remains uncertain whether Willy himself shares the insight.

In this early story Malamud has the kindly Mr. Panessa express a sentiment that can serve as a metaphor for Malamud's persistently expressed view of humans as sentient beings who need compassion and communion in the face of an often oppressive existence. Although on the edge of bankruptcy, the grocer extends credit to a poverty-stricken customer, saying that being human meant "you give credit to somebody else and he gave credit to you." To fail to give "credit" to another human being—even when you know the credit is undeserved—is to deny the humanity in yourself, to extinguish within your own being the light that has been given to you.

Malamud depicts down-and-out characters who try to salvage small victories from large defeats. Using ingenious symbols, and picturesque or grotesque characters, he ends his short stories with quick, mildly shocking conclusions: two men kissing, death chants for the living, reversals of victor and victim, the ascendence of a black Jewish angel, flashes of self-revelation. These frozen tableaux leave the reader slightly dazzled and bewildered. The apparent simplicity of Malamud's plots and the obviousness of his subject matter combine with the sophisticated techniques of the modern short-story writer to create a tension—an intricate interplay of form and content—that captures, when successful, a strangely haunting segment of human experience. In his parables of pain, suffering, and the possibility of moral growth, Malamud is able to touch the conscience and excite the visual imagination.

In "The Mourners" (1955), Kessler, a retired egg candler,* lives as a recluse in "a cheap flat on the top

---

*A person who holds a candle close to each egg to examine it for signs of fertilization.

floor of a decrepit tenement on the East Side," having long ago abandoned his wife and children. After an argument with the janitor over the disposal of the garbage, Kessler is given notice, but he refuses to leave. With the compassionate help of his neighbors, who are aroused by his suffering and loneliness, Kessler manages to cling to his "home." The landlord, Gruber, threatens Kessler with dispossession. Kessler responds by barricading himself inside his flat.

One day, overcome by apprehension at his tenant's silence, Gruber climbs the four flights of stairs to Kessler's apartment. Despite pangs of guilt, he plans to increase the rent after Kessler's eviction. When his loud knocking brings no response, Gruber nervously lets himself in with a passkey. He discovers Kessler sitting on the floor (a sign of mourning in Jewish tradition), "rocking back and forth," moaning and tearing at his flesh. Kessler is mourning for himself, his past misdeeds, his abandoned wife and children. But Gruber, "sweating brutally," suddenly conceives the notion that Kessler mourns for him, his dead spirit of humanity. He becomes filled with remorse for all the pain he has inflicted. "With a cry of shame he tore the sheet off Kessler's bed, and wrapping it around his bulk, sank heavily to the floor and became a mourner."

Within nine pages Malamud creates a strangely moving experience. The bleak setting of crumbling tenements and stinking apartments serves as an appropriate backdrop for Kessler's life of self-imposed loneliness and isolation. The conditions of his apartment parallel the rotting, disordered, aimless wreckage of his life. He is a grotesque character leading a grotesque life. And yet, by the end of the story Kessler arrives at a moral insight—and what is more, causes another, Gruber, to have a shock of ironic self-recognition.

Some critics have complained that the spectacular epiphany in which the two men join together in their repentance is too abrupt and weighted with meaning to be supported by such two-dimensional, grotesque characters. The criticism is certainly just. Here, even more than in his novels, Malamud strains the plot line in the direction of symbolic meanings. Nonetheless, "The Mourners" produces a haunting, disquieting reaction that stays with the reader long after the story is put aside. Malamud uses a spare, symbolic design that moves Kessler and Gruber from caricature to moral allegory. In the process he somehow creates a surprisingly full experience.

Several techniques of style contribute to this accomplishment. Gruber's speech is laced with colorful expressions that nicely capture his put-upon air of imposed burdens, as when he implores his janitor, "Don't monkey with my blood pressure." Malamud underscores Gruber's exaggerated air of suffering by using the language of hyperbole. When he receives bad news while eating dinner, "The food turned to lumps in his throat." When Gruber enters Kessler's apartment and sees him engaged in his act of mourning, he "gazed around the room, it was clean, drenched in daylight and fragrance." Bypassing realism, Malamud is better able to capture the moment of moral crisis, when Kessler and Gruber transcend their suffering by remembering (or discovering) their common humanity. Yet, ironically, Gruber's genuine and moving self-recognition comes from the mistaken impression that Kessler is mourning for him, when in fact Kessler mourns only his own past misdeeds. It is a moment of double self-discovery mixed with misapprehension, a powerful statement in irony that creates a bittersweet moment of pained possibility.

"Angel Levine" (1955) is less somber and more fantastic. Manischevitz, a poor Jewish tailor, under-

goes Job-like "reverses and indignities." He has lost
everything, business, son, daughter; he has a wife who
is hopelessly ill and Manischevitz is himself too sick to
work more than a few hours a day to maintain their
bare existence. In answer to his prayers, Levine arrives, a black Jewish angel who is "in a condition of
probation" until he can earn his wings through inspir-
ing the tailor's faith. Unable to accept the idea of a
Jewish angel being black, Manischevitz rejects him,
and both fall into deep despair. Finally, continued suffering causes the tailor to acknowledge Levine as "an
angel from God," whereupon Levine soars off to
heaven on "a pair of magnificent black wings" and
Manischevitz's troubles miraculously cease. "A
wonderful thing . . .," he tells his suddenly healthy
wife, "Believe me, there are Jews everywhere."

In this story Malamud uses fantasy as a unifying
frame for a mixture of the comic and the serious. The
reader must accept the story on three levels simultaneously—the real, the supernatural, and the allegorical. The matter-of-fact language has a rough-hewn
simplicity that convinces one of the reality of Manischevitz's suffering:

Fanny [his wife] lay at death's door. Through shrunken lips
she muttered concerning her childhood, the sorrows of the
marriage bed, the loss of her children, yet wept to live.
Manischevitz tried not to listen, but even without ears he
would have heard.

Although Levine claims to be an angel, he is described
in the language of everyday reality, so that the reader,
like Manischevitz, wonders how a spiritual being
could appear in such an earthy, slightly disheveled
form. Levine is a realistic angel, but he also has the
symbolic and allegorical function of a conscience
figure who provides Manischevitz with a test of faith.
In this way the story becomes a comic parable leading

to a moment of self-recognition for Manischevitz and moral awareness for the reader.

After first meeting Levine, Manischevitz wonders, "so if God sends me an angel, why a black?" He becomes convinced of Levine's legitimacy when he dreams of the black "standing before a faded mirror preening small decaying opalescent wings." He passes his test of faith by accepting Levine as a humane, compassionate, and possibly supernatural being and arrives at the insight that shows the point of the parable—"there are Jews everywhere." In other words, all men suffer, but we can transcend our suffering if we recognize and have faith in our common humanity.

Some commentators have maintained that the story is too fanciful and fantastic to be taken seriously. True, the presence of the supernatural is likely to puzzle the reader, but Malamud creates confusion deliberately for comic and thematic effect. For example, the final line about Jews being everywhere serves not only as an ironic, slightly enigmatic statement weighted with moral meaning, but also as a comic punchline that satirizes the myth of the Jews holding the patent on suffering. In addition, the fantastic comedy of the story implies the existence of a spiritual dimension in life without commiting Malamud to a specific faith, dogma, or theology.

"The Jewbird" (1963) is an even more bizarre fantasy, but in this case the central character fails his test of faith. Harry Cohen, a frozen-food salesman, unconsciously wishes to escape his Jewishness and become a fully assimilated American. His latent hatred of Jewishness becomes aroused when a talking bird—a Yiddish-speaking Jewbird called Mr. Schwartz—flies into his kitchen. Asking only for a place to stay, a little herring, maybe a glass of schnapps, Schwartz in return helps Harry's son with his schoolwork. In time, with his Yiddish speech and old-country ways Schwartz becomes a haunting reminder of Harry's immigrant experience. Harry becomes increasingly hostile to Schwartz and eventually throws him out the window into the winter snow, apparently killing him.

Clearly Schwartz serves as a symbolic character, a subconscious double who represents that part of Cohen, his Jewish identity, that he wishes to deny. Harry is a trapped and tortured character; his failure to accept the Jewbird represents a rejection of himself. "The Jewbird," like "Angel Levine," is an anecdote whose punchline provides the point of the comic parable: "Who did it to you, Mr. Schwartz?" asks the weeping son upon finding the frozen, mangled corpse. "Anti-Semeets," Mrs. Cohen says later. If "Angel Levine" suggests that Jews (metaphorically) are everywhere, "The Jewbird" demonstrates the opposite, that anti-Semites are everywhere; even a Jew can become one by denying a part of himself and losing his sense of humanity.

The story succeeds because of the matter-of-fact style with which Malamud treats the fantastic. "The window was open so the skinny bird flew in. Flappity-flap with its frazzled black wings. That's how it goes. It's open, you're in. Closed, you're out and that's your fate." The idiom is a terse, rapid vernacular that captures the rhythms of Yiddish combined with an ironic understatement. In addition, the differing speech patterns of Harry Cohen and Jewbird Schwartz reveal the central conflict between Jewish heritage and assimilationist ambition. Speaking of Cohen's son, Schwartz says, in Yiddish-English, "He's a good boy—you don't have to worry. He won't be a schicker [drunk] or a wifebeater, God forbid, but a scholar he'll never be, if you know what I mean, although maybe a good mechanic. It's no disgrace in these times." Harry replies in colloquial American, "If I were you . . . I'd keep

my big snoot out of other people's private business." As
Harry's antagonism climaxes, the two engage in a farcical wrestling match in which Schwartz catches
Harry's nose in his beak and Harry punches the bird
with his fist. If the style were more elaborate, the
whole thing would be only a gag using the comic
technique of incongruous juxtaposition. By maintain-
ing the contrast between the matter-of-fact, earthy
language and the fantastic events, Malamud creates a
comic parable whose silliness turns serious at the end.
The reader, by virtue of Cohen's failure to accept his
own buried genuine self, is given a glimpse of moral
insight into the painful duality of human nature.

In "Idiots First" (1963), the Angel of Death mate-
rializes as an arrogant, bulky figure named Ginzburg,
"with hairy nostrils and a fishy smell," who pursues a
dying Jew named Mendel. The action turns on Mendel's desperate determination to fend off his pursuer
until he can get his grown imbecile son, Isaac, on a
train to a California kinsman. His frantic efforts to
raise money for Isaac's fare culminate in violence
when Ginzburg, reappearing as the station ticket collector, informs the pleading father he has missed the
train, which Mendel can plainly see waiting at the
platform. "What will happen happens," Ginzburg
smirks. "This isn't my responsibility. . . . I ain't in the
anthropomorphic business." Nor, he adds, is pity his
"commodity." "The law is the law . . . the cosmic
universal law." Shouting, "You bastard, don't you
know what it means human?" Mendel seizes the collector by the throat, and, despite the freezing cold that
invades his body, refuses to release his grip. As the
gasping father clings to Ginzburg, he sees in the collector's eyes "the depth of his [own] terror." But Mendel
sees also that Ginzburg, staring into his eyes, has
glimpsed in them the depth of his own "awful wrath."
Angel or not, the collector beholds darkness and "a

shimmering, starry, blinding light" that astounds and shames him. "Who me?" Ginzburg asks and relinquishes his grip. Isaac is free to go.

The story is a virtual mini-drama of Malamud's themes of compassion, charity, and sacrifice. Mendel's outraged cry, "Don't you know what it means human?" protests a blighted universe, but nonetheless his demonstration of love does make a difference, and in the end neither the Angel of Death nor his "cosmic law" has proved a match for a dying father's love. This bizarre story suggests that humans can defy inevitability; even fate may be humanized and life snatched (if briefly) from death.

"Idiots First" succeeds because of Malamud's skillful blending of reality and dream, natural and supernatural. From the opening lines, when Mendel draws on his "cold embittered clothing," reality becomes shaped by human feeling. As Mendel scurries about frantically trying to raise the train fare, the reality of the New York City setting on a bleak November night slowly slips away and becomes transformed into a vaguely surrealistic dream landscape of dark, deserted streets. At one point Mendel enters a strange park with leafless trees and a mournful wind, where he encounters a mysterious stranger whom he perceives to be Ginzburg. Unlike "The Mourners," in which Malamud puts a grotesque character into a realistic setting, in "Idiots First" he places comparatively real characters into a grotesque setting. The effect produces a disquieting blurring of the line between reality and fantasy. We do not know how much of the action "really" happens and how much exists in Mendel's desperately fearful imagination. The epiphany produces a shock that slowly turns to admiration as we realize we have before us a seriocomic parable of human pain and possibility.

In Malamud's most well known and perhaps best

story, "The Magic Barrel" (1954), Leo Finkle, an ascetic, scholarly rabbinical student nearing gradua-tion, decides to acquire a wife. He calls in a marriage broker, Pinye Salzman, who promises the timid Leo results from the photographs and information cards kept in a barrel. One prospect, Lily Hirschorn, asks how he became "enamored of God," and the potential rabbi unconsciously blurts, "I came to God not be-cause I loved Him, but because I did not." This brief encounter proves to be a soul-shattering experience, as Leo comes to the unexpected realization that he can-not love God because he does not love humanity. However, he guiltily consoles himself that "he was a Jew and a Jew suffered"—and if he is imperfect, his ideal is not. He feels that this new self-knowledge will help him find a bride.

His hopes quickly fade; most of Pinye's photo-graphed faces bear the marks of defeat. Yet the final one, a girl whose face seems to reflect both youth and age, innocence and experience, touches his heart. If Pinye is delighted at the prospect of a commission, he is horrified at Leo's choice. Her picture was a mistake, he protests. The girl is Pinye's own daughter, Stella, "a wild one." "To me she is dead now," Pinye declares. But Leo insists. This girl will understand him—per-haps even love him. "He . . . concluded to convert her to goodness, himself to God." Yet when the old man finally agrees, Leo suspects a well-laid trap. Stella awaits him under a street lamp wearing a white dress and red shoes. As Leo rushes toward her, he notes that her eyes are "filled with desperate innocence," and he pictures in her "his own redemption." Around the cor-ner the old marriage broker leans against the wall chanting prayers for the dead.

The events of the story force Leo to realize that his years of isolated study have served largely as an escape from life. His attraction to Stella derives from his belief that she has lived, has experienced the pain of life and yet has retained a kind of innocence. When he meets her she wears scarlet for prostitution and white for purity. The ambiguous concluding tableau does not reveal whether Leo has headed towards salvation or destruction.

Speaking a colorful Yiddishized English and reeking of fish, Pinye Salzman is half con-man and half spiritual exemplar. Each of the marital candidates sounds like a used car for which Pinye makes a "pitch." When Leo meets Lily Hirschorn, he realizes that both of them have been "sold a bill of goods." She is older than he thought; he is not the "wonder rabbi" she had expected. Yet, as Lily's questions force him to a moment of profound self-illumination, Leo has the strange sense that Pinye lurks nearby, "perhaps in a tree . . . , flashing the lady signals with a pocket mirror." After he has fallen in love with Stella from her picture, Leo is "afflicted by a tormenting suspicion that Salzman had planned it all to happen this way." The reader, like Leo, is left wondering whether Pinye is merely a clever con-man or a spiritual teacher.

Pinye's earthy speech and high-pressure sale's techniques create a comic contrast to Leo's learning and innocence. Pinye also contrasts in another way— he serves as a representative of the traditional, old-country way of life, an ethos that is fast disappearing in modern America. The old man is astonished to hear the young rabbinical student from Cleveland launch into a learned discourse on the time-honored institution of the arranged marriage. However, Leo reveals his true feelings when he rejects Pinye's final, and most attractive, candidate: "'Ruth K. Nineteen years. Honor student. Father offers thirteen thousand cash to the right bridegroom. He is a medical doctor. Stomach specialist with marvelous practice. Brother in law owns garment business. Particular people.' . . . 'But

don't you think this young girl believes in love?' " A
fear of life and love, not a pious sense of tradition has
led Leo to the old matchmaker. Yet Pinye serves as
counterpart as well as contrast to Leo. He is a subconscious double who represents a submerged part of
Leo's soul that he cannot ignore. Dogged by the wily
old man, Leo learns that life consists of more than
book learning. In this way Pinye serves as the catalyst
for Leo to gain insight into himself.

In a nearly perfect union of form and content,
Malamud uses fantasy and the changing of the seasons
to create a unifying frame for this comic parable of
denial of life and the hope of regeneration. Malamud
structures the actions of the story around the symbolic
association of spring with hope and regeneration.
Leo's pain and isolation occur in winter; with spring
comes the incident with Lily and the possibility of a
new life. Leo's painful self-insight amounts to the
labor pains of his emotional rebirth.

More remarkable is the language through which
Malamud infuses the story with fantasy. At the moment of Leo's insight into his lack of love, he looks at
the sky and sees "a profusion of loaves of bread go flying like ducks over his head." Malamud captures
Pinye's plaintive frustration at Leo's indecisiveness by
describing him as "a skeleton with haunted eyes"; hurt
by Leo's rejection of him "Salzman's face went dead
white, the world had snowed on him." When Leo
meets Stella, Malamud writes, "he pictured, in her, his
own redemption. Violins and lit candles revolved in
the sky." The careful phrasing of the first of these two
sentences makes clear that the optimism belongs to
Leo and may or may not be shared by Malamud; the
second sentence contains no definite indication
whether the vision of violins and candles in the sky exists only in Leo's mind; this ambiguity causes a blurring of the lines between fact and fantasy.

The concluding picture of Pinye chanting the prayer for the dead (kaddish) uses realistic language but occurs within the context of fantasy. The effect is to produce a striking but deliberately ambiguous ending. In Jewish tradition a man may chant kaddish for a living relative as a means of symbolically disowning that person. In a general sense, kaddish may simply suggest great sorrow. Does Pinye mourn simply because his daughter is dead to him? Or does he mourn for himself because of his complicity in bringing Leo and Stella together? Or, perhaps, for Leo's loss of innocence? Or Stella's sinful ways? All (and more) are possible. The ironic juxtaposition of hopeful optimism with unexpected sorrow, all within a context of fantasy, suggests the inappropriateness of a literal interpretation. The reader is left with the illogical, vaguely unsettling but deeply moving impression that Pinye's mournful chant somehow captures the pain, suffering, and loneliness of life while also welcoming the possibility of spiritual growth.

"The Silver Crown" (1972) features another pair of memorable characters. Albert Gans, a high school chemistry teacher whose father is dying of cancer, visits a faith healer, Rabbi Jonas Lifschitz, a down-to-earth, homey Jew smelling of old age, who unabashedly mixes the idiom of religion with the materialistic concerns of a charlatan. The doubtful, scientifically trained American agrees to have the healer prepare a crown of melted silver dollars designed and blessed in a way that can miraculously restore health. Lifschitz assures him that the crown must be made "individual for your father. Then his health will be restored. There are two prices—." Albert impulsively orders the more expensive crown, but after paying $986 he suffers a change of heart and decides that he has been tricked by a clever confidence man using hypnosis. Rushing back to Lifschitz's dingy

apartment, Albert demands the return of his money.
"Be merciful . . .," implores Lifschitz, "Think of your
father who loves you." "He hates me," Albert retorts,
"the son of a bitch, I hope he croaks." As if in response
to his son's denunciation, the elder Gans "an hour
later . . . shut his eyes and expired."

The reader learns at the outset what Albert
himself cannot acknowledge—that his desperate attempt to do something for his father stems from guilt
at having previously neglected him. Unable to decide
whether or not this "wonder rabbi" is a charlatan,
Albert vacillates between the yearning to believe and
the fear of making a fool of himself. But Rabbi Jonas
Lifschitz remains an enigma. The reader no more
knows how to interpret his words than Albert does. At
one point Malamud does reveal the old man's
thoughts. Upon first meeting Albert Lifschitz sizes him
up as the "crafty type. . . . Him I have to watch
myself with." The Yiddish voice helps characterize the
rabbi as an old-world type, but beyond that the reader
remains in the dark. Lifschitz's suspiciousness,
however, echoes Albert's and produces an intriguing
comic effect of opposing possibilities: is he suspicious
because he is a fake, fearful of exposure, or because he
is a genuine healer, concerned for the elder Gans's
well-being?

The reader never learns whether Jonas Lifschitz
believes in his own powers or is simply a clever con-
man. But it is he who gives voice to the story's spiritual
truths. When Albert asks whether he must believe in
the crown's power in order for it to work, the rabbi
replies that everyone has doubts: "We doubt God and
God doubts us. . . . I am not afraid so long as you love
your father." Love and compassion, in other words,
can help overcome the uncertainty of life. Without
them spiritual growth is impossible. Albert fails his test
of faith because he does not love. In the end it is he

who reveals himself as the charlatan whose self-deception possibly has prevented a miracle.

Using a narrative style that tightly interlocks the real and the imaginary, "The Silver Crown" captures modern man's ambivalence towards miracles in the face of increasing secularism and the attendant suspiciousness towards spiritual claims. Against an indistinct background of battered synagogues, rundown stores, ramshackle apartments, and Albert's general concern about "the war, atom bomb, pollution, death . . . ," the story comments on the universal oppositions of spirituality vs. materialism, belief vs. doubt, commitment vs. withdrawal. The reader's confusion about what is real and what is hallucination mounts when Albert demands to see a sample crown. Lifschitz reluctantly agrees and tells Albert to look into the mirror, where he sees "a crown of rare beauty" whose image "lasted no more than five short seconds, then the reflecting glass by degrees turned dark and empty."

Albert's vision in this "ghostly mirror" provides the central image for his divided soul. In a similar way, most of Malamud's stories capture the ambivalence of human nature by using techniques that allow the characters to see themselves. Self-appraisal may come from dreams, visions, or visitations, or it may come from such refractive surfaces as mirrors, photographs, and the human eye, all of which serve to confront people with their inner compulsions, passions, and frustrations.

Not all of Malamud's stories take place in an immigrant milieu. Young Americans in Italy and struggling artists or writers also appear frequently. In many of his stories Malamud also experiments with new themes and techniques. Nonetheless, Jews living on New York's East Side provide his favorite setting and subject. From this background Malamud creates his best stories and his distinctive literary vision. Drawing upon recollections of a folk culture that has virtually disappeared in America, Malamud universalizes the Jewish immigrant experience, creating characters who meet their crises with tremendous vitality. He uses his inventiveness in fantasy to explore the relationship between tragedy and comedy, fantasy and reality, art and life.

In his comic and seriocomic parables of human pain and possibility, Malamud demonstrates a commitment to suffering human beings in their painfully absurd condition. No matter how pathetic or foolish, the individual can, Malamud insists, assert his humanity. Malamud's stories are seldom profound or complex; by insisting on presenting moral truths, he dares to be old-fashioned. Almost trite, almost sentimental, his stories manage to touch the soul. Painted on a small canvas with a limited number of strokes and colors—carefully chosen and skillfully executed— Malamud's odd tales of fateful small happenings move the spirit and haunt the imagination. Provoking a sudden shock of insight, often cloaked in protective irony, the story ends, and the world goes on its way.

# 10

••••••••••••••••••••••••••••••••••••••••••••••••••••••

# Malamud's Moral
# and Artistic Vision

Critics have thoroughly evaluated Malamud's work.
Because his gift is multifaceted, different critics emphasize different aspects of his fiction. Jonathan
Baumbach discusses Malamud as fantasist; F. W.
Dupee evaluates him as a realist; Earl Wasserman
writes of Malamud as symbolist; Charles Alva Hoyt
and Jackson Benson explore Malamud's American
romanticism; Robert Ducharme and Max Schultz examine his mythic technique; Earl Rovit treats him as a
writer in the Jewish folk tradition; Ruth R. Wisse and
Leslie A. Field examine Malamud's uses of the
schlemiel; Sheldon Grebstein analyzes stylistic innova-
tions. Most critics mention Malamud's humor and
irony, as well as his humanistic affirmation and ethical
concern. His mastery of ironic plotting and effect, his
distinctive techniques and forms combine with his
compassion for humanity and moral purpose to produce a complex vision of muted belief in the potential
of the human spirit.

Regardless of each critic's particular interest in
Malamud's fiction, virtually all agree that the most
noticeable component is its moral vision. As a
humanist, Malamud is committed to a position that is
neither wholly Jewish, nor Christian, nor existential.
Because his statements of moral purpose do not mention God, it seems safe to conclude that he does not
believe in a supernatural deity, as such. Nor does his
work fall within the Greek and Christian tradition of

tragedy. However, in his writing Malamud draws on his understanding of all these traditions.

Early in his writing career, Malamud began to combine his humanistic moral vision with a sense of ethnic identity to create what might be called a "Jewish" humanism. The fusion of his moral concerns with the colorful ethnicity and ironic humor of immigrant Jews produced a distinctly urban comic vision that freed Malamud's inventiveness and his talent for fantasy without compromising his moral earnestness. The combination is so fortuitous that throughout his career Malamud has continued to explore the artistic possibilities of this vision. Drawing on his childhood memories of Yiddish-speaking Americans in New York City, Malamud created a whole arsenal of narrative and stylistic techniques that adapt the rhythms of Yiddish, a folktale-like use of fantasy, and the double vision of Jewish humor.

Writing in a parable mode that uses (to varying degrees) his own distinctive mix of realism, myth, fantasy, romance, comedy, and fairy tale, Malamud has continued to grow artistically. Always a writer willing to take risks, he has freely experimented with new themes and techniques, especially in his short stories. He has over the years developed considerable stylistic range and has often attempted to move beyond the pale of his "Jewish" humanism. These efforts are always interesting, frequently successful. Yet his great achievement, as an artist and as a moralist, has come from his success in creating a distinctive fictional world that is the embodiment of his "Jewish" humanism.

Central to Malamud's moral sensibility is his positive, pragmatic attitude toward suffering. When asked about suffering as a subject in his writing, Malamud replied, "I'm against it, but when it occurs why waste the experience?" His fiction suggests that life—at least for goodhearted, humane people—is a search to make unavoidable suffering meaningful. Nearly all of his novels center on the suffering that results from the conflict between human freedom and human limitations, with the stress on the latter rather than the former. Frank Alpine (*The Assistant*), Sy Levin (*A New Life*), Yakov Bok (*The Fixer*), Arthur Fidelman (*Pictures of Fidelman*), Roy Hobbs (*The Natural*), and Harry Lesser (*The Tenants*), all strive to escape an ignominious or unfulfilling past and to achieve a new life of comfort and fulfillment. All six are defeated in their ambition, but the first four achieve a new dignity, turning defeat into victory by assuming a burden of self-sacrifice. Frank Alpine assumes the living death of the deceased Morris Bober—running Morris's store and assuming the responsibility for his family—out of a deepened sense of commitment mixed with a sense of guilt and a vague hope of winning the love of Morris's daughter. Yakov Bok chooses prison over release for the sake of all Russian Jews. Sy Levin achieves a kind of unsought-after heroism by sacrificing his career for the principle of love, accepting responsibility for a love he no longer feels. Arthur Fidelman learns self-sacrifice born of love and compassion. Roy Hobbs, on the other hand, fails to learn from his suffering and yields to materialism by accepting a bribe (although the ending hints that he may now be able to begin a new life with Iris Lemon). Harry Lesser shuts himself off from humanity in a misguided attempt to achieve artistic self-actualization.

Malamud characteristically develops the idea of the regenerative power of suffering by using the Jew (specifically the schlemiel figure) as a symbol of conscience and moral behavior. In *The Assistant*, Frank Alpine comes to believe that, as a Jew, Morris Bober lives in order to suffer, but Morris tells him that we all

suffer because we all live—it is one of the conditions of
life. A Jew, Morris says, suffers for the Law, and the
Law is "to do what is right, to be honest, to be good."
After he accepts the burden of Morris's suffering,
Frank Alpine's conversion to Judaism is merely the appropriate symbolic action—perhaps heavy-handed in
its symbolism—to complete the statement of the novel.
Yet the act does grow naturally from Frank's
understanding of what it means to be a Jew—an
understanding that is much like Malamud's own view
of Jewishness as an avenue to the goals of humanism.[1]
In a celebrated statement, Malamud once said, "All
men are Jews except they don't know it."[2] By this he
meant that the Jew can serve to represent the individual's existential situation as an isolated, displaced
loner who has the potential for achieving moral
transcendence through suffering that engenders insight and a commitment to love. All people, Malamud
implies, have a common identity as ethical beings; for
example, by the end of *The Assistant*, Frank Alpine
has learned that indeed, metaphorically, "All men are
Jews."

In Malamud's fiction, the Jew as a symbol of
ethical man is joined by another pervasive symbol—that of life as a prison. When Morris Bober
resents his bad fortune, he sees his grocery store as a
"prison," a "graveyard," a "tomb." The store is the
source of his bitterness, suffering, and frustration—
evidence of the limitations of the human condition on
earth—and at the same time it symbolizes Morris's
very existence, embodying the source of his moral
strength. *A New Life* moves Malamud even closer to
an explicit existentialist viewpoint. Sy Levin chooses a
future "chained" to Pauline Gilley. With her he might
appear to be a free man, but really he will be locked
inside "a windowless prison" that is "really himself,
flawed ediface of failures, each locking up tight the

one before." In other words, Levin has exercised the
freedom to choose his own "prison." Similarly, Yakov
Bok finds spiritual peace only after choosing to remain
in the tsar's prison, with no guarantee of ever being
released. Harry Lesser voluntarily entombs himself in
what he likes to think of as a "sacred cathedral" of art,
but which turns out to be the prison of his own divided
soul.

Yet one must ask whether Malamud's metaphoric
use of the Jew to represent the good man struggling for
a meaningful existence in the prison of life is convincing. Certainly the European Jews, throughout the
Middle Ages and again in the nineteenth and twentieth centuries, experienced an extraordinary amount
of suffering, but in elevating their hardship to the level
of an ethical symbol, Malamud, in spite of his characteristic irony, sometimes borders on sentimentality.
For example, near the end of *The Fixer* Yakov Bok's
lawyer proclaims to his client, "You suffer for us
all. . . . I would be honored to be in your place." Seen
in this light, Malamud's famous statement, "All men
are Jews," implies that it is the human lot to suffer,
that suffering is potentially beneficial, and that we
should therefore learn to accept our burdens and see in
them the promise of growth and fulfillment.

Critics often talk about the theme of redemptive
suffering in Malamud's works. This terminology can
be misleading, since it has the effect of suggesting a
specifically Christian view of salvation that is present
but peripheral in Malamud's fiction. It should be emphasized that his vision has its roots in the Old Testament, while the Christian idea of salvation derives
from the New Testament. This point is fundamental to
an understanding of Malamud's work. In his fiction,
he unrelentingly asks what might be called Old Testament questions: Why do good men suffer while evil
men frequently prosper? Why should we be good,

when there is no reward for goodness? How can we have faith when there are no signs to confirm our faith? Why should we love, if our love is met only with scorn? Malamud's perspective on these age-old questions is heavily influenced by the somewhat fatalistic Old Testament story of Job, a pious man who suffers unjustly without ever understanding why. He knows only that it is God's will that he suffer. To the man who suffers without any apparent reason, God's ways seem harsh and unjust, but Job does not attempt to rationalize this injustice; rather, he acknowledges this as part of the mystery of life. It is simply the way of the world; the sun shines as brightly on the wicked as it does on the good and just.

The suffering of Morris Bober and Yakov Bok is not redemptive in the Christian sense. For them as Jews, the concepts of heaven and hell do not offer a solution to the dilemma of existence. They have no sense of individual salvation; they do not believe that their suffering in this life will be rewarded in the next. Malamud's view is rather that goodness is its own reward while evil inflicts its own punishment. This is why love and compassion—and schlemiel heroes—are so important in Malamud's fiction. No suffering can be redeemed by any act of God or the State. The only "solution" possible for the problem of evil is for people to respect and nourish each other now, during this life. And only a schlemiel would choose the intangible spiritual rewards of goodness over the material benefits of narrow self-interest. Thus, Malamud's association of suffering with Jewishness is not merely sentimental. It also contains a hardheaded realism.

Suffering, however, does not interest Malamud for its own sake. It is, rather, a corollary to his real concern, one that can easily be missed: what he primarily wishes to explore and express is the sheer terror of existence in the twentieth century. The horrors of

Verdun, the Great Depression, Dresden, Auschwitz, Hiroshima, Vietnam—the world's "uncertain balance of terror," as President Kennedy expressed it in his inaugural address—these have their counterparts in Malamud's fiction. Backdrops of Depression hardship, symbolic landscapes of garbage-filled back alleys and collapsing buildings, McCarthyism, and anti-Semitic injustice on a massive scale—these settings cast their dark shadows over all of Malamud's fictional world, serving as constant reminders that we are faced with malevolent forces so powerful that they threaten our very existence as thinking, feeling, moral beings. Thus it was understandable that Malamud should choose the Jews as symbols of suffering, for they have lived through the Holocaust, the most horrifying campaign of terror in human history. In Malamud's works the Jew becomes an isolated loner who represents the hopes, fears, and possibilities of twentieth-century humanity.

Suffering in Malamud's fiction, then, has two aspects, one somewhat sentimental, the other more fatalistic, full of terror. To the extent that Malamud's writing romanticizes suffering, it is dangerous and destructive. Morris Bober and Frank Alpine are masterful creations, but for people actually to submit to similar suffering in their own lives, acting on the belief that their suffering will somehow redeem them, would be fruitless and masochistic. Similarly, Yakov Bok becomes a powerful example of a human being's ability to grow spiritually in the face of injustice, but the hard fact is that most poor people unjustly imprisoned—even "political prisoners"—simply waste away without ever being allowed to serve the cause of justice, no matter how noble their suffering might be. But Malamud surely never intended anyone to take his metaphoric treatment of suffering literally, as a life model. Nonetheless, the literal implication is there.

For the most part, however, the hardheaded attitude toward suffering prevails in Malamud's fiction. In this respect his writing provides a sort of strategy for living with the terror of modern life on an everyday basis. This is the source of both the power and the importance of his fiction. *The Assistant* and *The Fixer* are Malamud's strongest novels largely because they capture most effectively our existential sense of terror in the modern world.

Another source of power in Malamud's writing lies in the special relationship he creates between pairs of characters. One often thinks of his characters as coming in sets—Frank Alpine and Morris Bober, Harry Lesser and Willie Spearmint, Fidelman and Susskind, Finkle and Salzman, Gruber and Kessler, Mendel and Ginzburg, Harry Cohen and "Jewbird" Schwartz, Manischevitz and (Angel) Levine, Albert Gans and Rabbi Jonas Lifschitz. In general, one of three different kinds of relationship binds each pair together.

The first involves a character near the protagonist who represents his conscience and who, ultimately, challenges his humanity. The prototype is Susskind in "Last Mohican." Trying mightily to escape Susskind's "harassment," Fidelman simply cannot avoid the inevitable confrontation, for Susskind echoes a lost part of Fidelman, of his heritage and his conscience. He is forced, through Susskind's uncanny ability to track him down, to take inventory of his soul and to come to terms with himself. In this way Malamud uses Susskind and other symbolic conscience figures such as Morris Bober, Shmuel, and "Jewbird" Schwartz to dramatize the respective protagonist's spiritual conflict.

The relentless pursuit of one character by another in Malamud's fiction operates as a symbolic double image, representing two contradictory tendencies in each of us, the urge to flee and the determination to fight. The secret escapist urge to remain uninvolved with life competes with the call (often prompted by guilt) to a conscious and willed acceptance of responsibility.

The second kind of relationship that binds pairs of characters together, sometimes overlapping with the first, depends on a more destructive psychological process; namely, symbiotic victimization—the intense, often irrational relationship of two people who are bound together by a strange mixture of hate and compassion, intolerance and understanding, guilt and forgiveness, each needing the other in some way to achieve completeness.

The prototype for these symbiotic pairs appears in the early story, "The Death of Me," which was first published in 1951 and later collected in *Idiots First.* Marcus, a tailor, has two assistants who both are fond of Marcus but despise each other for apparently complex reasons that Marcus cannot fully understand. Their feuding eventually erupts into a serious fight, in which the combatants injure each other with makeshift weapons. But they are not the only ones to suffer. Marcus becomes so upset by the atmosphere of dissension that he has a heart attack and dies. Malamud emphasizes the effects of the mutual hatred rather than probing deeply into its causes. "The Death of Me" portrays the same kind of larger moral consequence Malamud emphasizes in *The Tenants*, where Levenspiel and Irene—indeed, all of us—suffer from Harry and Willie's mutual self-destruction. The theme of symbiotic victimization describes the failure of men to nourish and sustain each other in the face of the terror of existence. In "The Mourners," for example, the ironic ending turns on the reader's awareness that Gruber and Kessler remain isolated from each other in spite of their individual flashes of self-awareness.

The third kind of relationship draws its power from the primacy of family relationships; its impulse lies in the search for a father. Many of Malamud's protagonists are orphans (actual or symbolic), unconsciously searching for the male parent they lost or never had. Frank Alpine, Sy Levin, Yakov Bok, and Arthur Fidelman all receive nourishment and a degree of wisdom or compassion by accepting a surrogate father. Roy Hobbs, on the other hand, rejects the fatherly influence of Pop Fisher and suffers a moral defeat in so doing.

Although many cultures have legends and myths about orphans in search of fathers, Malamud's use of the theme, like his attitude toward suffering, has its roots firmly embedded in the Old Testament. Central to an understanding of the Old Testament as a Jewish epic history is the idea of the Jews as God's Chosen People. The patriarchal monotheism of the Jews derives from the conception of God as a stern father who made a covenant with the Hebrews to be their God if they would agree to worship him alone and to obey his commandments. This covenant was first entered into by the patriarch Abraham and later renewed by his heirs, Isaac and Jacob. However, being chosen was a mixed blessing, for failure to live up to God's high ethical standards brought frequent punishment and suffering to the Hebrews. As a result, the Jews, historically, developed a very special relationship with their God; bitterness and even hatred resided alongside praise and thankfulness. Strangely, to modern theism, the relationship was reciprocal: God needed the Jews almost as much as they needed him, because, according to Jewish folklore, although he had previously approached many other tribes with the offer of the holy contract, none but the Jews would accept his commandments.

In Malamud's writing, the archetypal theme of

the search for a father has a spiritual dimension. Its prototype is the ancient Hebrews' relationship with their God. This special biblical influence is most explicitly revealed in "Angel Levine," where Manischevitz must set aside his prejudices and be able to believe in Levine before the angel can perform a miracle. In accepting a spiritual father, Frank Alpine, Sy Levin, Yakov Bok, and Arthur Fidelman reenact Abraham's entering into a sacred covenant, which gives their lives an ethical meaning and provides them with a new sense of identity.

In his fiction Malamud considers the moral evolution of his characters. They grow in ethical depth through various kinds of suffering, intellectual as well as physical. Using such techniques as mirror images, symbiotic pairs of characters, and the double vision of Jewish humor, Malamud often succeeds in showing us the human soul, stripped bare of romantic dreams, pretense, and materialistic aspirations, in conflict with its own divided nature. It is no exaggeration to say that spiritual conflict dwells at the center of Malamud's moral universe. Freedom can be achieved, but only through moral awareness, which, paradoxically, binds a person to others in a web of commitments.

Each of the protagonists of Malamud's novels faces a trial of conscience or a spiritual test and triumphs only by accepting fatherly spiritual guidance or by listening to his own troubled conscience, an acceptance that must be accompanied by an expression of mercy, love, charity, or forgiveness. The three who pass the test—Frank Alpine, Sy Levin, and Yakov Bok—first find themselves in a desperate situation, try to escape, seek for justification, and reassure themselves about redemption. Their final experience, however, is purification, as they realize that justification for their actions will not come from God or any other external source—only from inside themselves.

Weighed down by self-doubts, internal conflicts, and the corrupting temptation to seek material success, Alpine, Levin, and Bok each nonetheless wins a moral victory.

The implied lesson is, quite simply, that people can change. Their circumstances may remain the same but spiritually they transcend their surroundings. This recurring theme in Malamud's writing is simple but efficacious. For example, as a corollary Malamud implies that life is relative. A store can become a prison for one man and a means of deliverance for another. Things, in and of themselves, are neither good nor bad; they are what we make of them. In the world of Malamud's fiction compassion, love, and understanding—the humane values—rather than physical circumstances give meaning to one's life. It is a world that blends hope with despair, pain with possibility, and suffering with moral growth. Out of the everyday defeats and indignities of ordinary people, Malamud creates beautiful parables that capture the joy as well as the pain of life; he expresses the dignity of the human spirit searching for freedom and moral growth in the face of hardship, injustice, and the existential anguish of life in our time.

# Notes

### 1. THE WRITER AS MORAL ACTIVIST

1. The address is printed in its entirety in *Writing in America*, John Fisher and Robert B. Silvers, eds. (New Brunswick, N.J.: Rutgers University Press, 1960), p. 173.
2. Walter Allen, *The Modern Novel in Britain and the United States* (New York: E. P. Dutton, 1964), p. 322.
3. Interview with Joseph Wershba, "Not Horror but Sadness," New York *Post* (14 September 1958), p. 172.
4. Quoted in *Current Biography Yearbook, 1958*, Marjoree Dent Cadee, ed. (New York, 1958), p. 272.
5. Philip Roth, "Writing American Fiction," *Commentary* (March 1961), p. 228.
6. Interview with Leslie A. and Joyce W. Field in *Bernard Malamud: A Collection of Critical Essays*, Leslie A. and Joyce W. Field, eds. (Englewood Cliffs, N.J.: Prentice-Hall, 1975), p. 8.
7. In addition to sources already cited, biographical information comes from interviews with Haskel Frankel, *Saturday Review* (10 September 1966), pp. 39–40, and Daniel Stern, *Paris Review* (Spring 1975), pp. 40–64, and Ralph Tyler, *New York Times Book Review* (18 February 1979), pp. 1ff.
8. *Current Biography Yearbook*, p. 272.
9. Henry James, preface to *The Americans*, quoted by Richard Chase, *The American Novel and Its Tradition* (Garden City, N.Y.: Doubleday, 1957), p. 25.
10. *Paris Review*, p. 56.
11. Although existentialism has been called a philosophical school, the existentialists themselves differ markedly in doctrine and attitude. Since World War II, there have been two major streams of existentialist thought. The Christian existentialism of Sören Kierkegaard, Karl Barth, and Paul Tillich has had little direct influence on

literature. The existentialism of Jean-Paul Sartre and
Martin Heidegger, on the other hand, has provided an
orientation for such literary figures as Albert Camus,
Simone de Beauvoir, and Sartre himself. Many existentialist writers look also for literary inspiration to the
works of Dostoevsky and Kafka, often considered analo-
gous in their philosophical outlook. It is to this latter
branch of existentialism—associated directly with the
philosophy of Sartre and indirectly with the fiction of
Dostoevsky, Kafka, and Camus—that my generaliza-
tions are intended to apply.

12. Many critics have mentioned Malamud's debt to ex-
istentialism. See in particular: Jerry Bryant, *The Open
Decision—The Contemporary American Novel and Its
Intellectual Background* (New York: Free Press, 1970);
Ihab Hassan, *Radical Innocence: Studies in the Con-
temporary American Novel* (Princeton, N.J.: Princeton
University Press, 1961); Alan Friedman, "The Hero as
Schnook," in *Bernard Malamud and the Critics*, Leslie
A. and Joyce W. Field, eds. (New York: New York Uni-
versity Press, 1970), pp. 285–303.

## 2.    THE HERO IN THE MODERN WORLD:
### *The Natural*

1. Leslie Fiedler, *The Jew in the American Novel* (New
York: Herzl Institute Pamphlet No. 10, 1959), p. 57.
2. According to Jessie Weston in *From Ritual to Romance*
(1920) the mythical patterns of the medieval Grail quest
evolved from primitive fertility rituals associated with
the natural cycle of the seasons. Weston found an archetypal fertility myth in the story of the Fisher King,
whose death, sickness, or impotence brings drought and
desolation to the land and its inhabitants. This mythical
pattern is discernible in stories of a dying god who is
later resurrected.
3. See Richard Chase, *The American Novel and Its Tradition* (Garden City, N.Y.: Doubleday, 1957).

4. Sidney Richman, *Bernard Malamud* (New York: Twayne Publishers, 1966), p. 46.

## 4. THE SCHLEMIEL OUT WEST: *A New Life*

1. Ruth B. Mandel, "Ironic Affirmation," in *Bernard Malamud and the Critics*, Leslie A. and Joyce W. Field, eds. (New York: New York University Press, 1970), p. 269.
2. This view has been convincingly argued by Robert Ducharme in *Art and Idea in the Novels of Bernard Malamud* (The Hague, Holland: Mouton & Co., 1974). In the following discussion, I am indebted to Ducharme's provocative ideas.
3. Richard Astro, "In the Heart of the Valley: Bernard Malamud's *A New Life* in *Bernard Malamud and the Critics*, p. 143.
4. Leslie Fiedler, "The Many Names of S. Levin: An Essay in Genre Criticism," in *The Fiction of Bernard Malamud*, Richard Astro and Jackson J. Benson, eds. (Corvallis: Oregon State University Press, 1977), p. 154.

## 5. ALIENATION AND AGGRESSION: *The Fixer*

1. Malamud interview with Haskel Frankel, *Saturday Review* (10 September 1966), p. 39.
2. Quoted in Granville Hicks, "One Man to Stand for Six Million," *Saturday Review* (10 September 1966), p. 38.

## 6. THE ARTIST AS SCHLEMIEL: *Pictures of Fidelman: An Exhibition*

1. Sheldon Grebstein, "Bernard Malamud and the Jewish Movement," in *Bernard Malamud: A Collection of Critical Essays*, Leslie A. and Joyce W. Field, eds.

(Englewood Cliffs, N.J.: Prentice-Hall, 1975), p. 43.
2.  Quoted in Ihab Hassan, "The Hopes of Man," *New York Times Book Review* (13 October, 1963), p. 5.


## 8.   A NEW LIFE REVISITED: *Dubin's Lives*

1.  Interview with Ralph Tyler, *New York Times Book Review*, 18 February 1979, p. 32.
2.  Interview with Ralph Tyler, p. 30.


## 10.   MALAMUD'S MORAL AND ARTISTIC VISION

1.  Letter to Sidney Richman reported in his *Bernard Malamud* (New York: Twayne Publishers, 1966), p. 146, n. 6.
2.  *Jerusulem Post* (Weekly Overseas Edition, 1 April 1968), p. 13.

# Bibliography

## 1. WORKS BY BERNARD MALAMUD

*The Natural.* New York: Harcourt, Brace, 1952.
*The Assistant.* New York: Farrar, Straus & Cudahy, 1957.
*The Magic Barrel.* New York: Farrar, Straus & Cudahy, 1958.
*A New Life.* New York: Farrar, Straus & Cudahy, 1961.
*Idiots First.* New York: Farrar, Straus, 1963.
*The Fixer.* New York: Farrar, Straus & Giroux, 1966.
*Pictures of Fidelman: An Exhibition.* New York: Farrar, Straus & Giroux, 1969.
*The Tenants.* New York: Farrar, Straus, & Giroux, 1971.
*Rembrandt's Hat.* New York: Farrar, Straus & Giroux, 1973.
*Dubin's Lives.* New York: Farrar, Straus & Giroux, 1979.

## 2. BOOKS ABOUT BERNARD MALAMUD

Astro, Richard, and Jackson J. Benson, eds. *The Fiction of Bernard Malamud.* American Authors Series. Corvallis: Oregon State University Press, 1977.

Cohen, Sandy. *Bernard Malamud and the Trial by Love.* Amsterdam: Rodopi N. V., 1974.

Ducharme, Robert. *Art and Idea in the Novels of Bernard Malamud.* The Hague, Holland: Mouton and Co., 1974.

Field, Leslie A. and Joyce W., eds. *Bernard Malamud and the Critics.* New York: New York University Press, 1970.

_____. *Bernard Malamud: A Collection of Critical Essays.* Twentieth Century Views. Englewood Cliffs, N.J.: Prentice-Hall, 1975.

Meeter, Glenn. *Bernard Malamud and Philip Roth: A Critical Essay.* Contemporary Writers in Christian Perspective Series. Grand Rapids, Mich.: William Eerdmans, 1968.

Richman, Sidney. *Bernard Malamud*. U.S. Authors Series. New York: Twayne Publishers, 1966.


### 3. ESSAYS ABOUT BERNARD MALAMUD

Alter, Robert. "Bernard Malamud: Jewishness as Metaphor." *After the Tradition: Essays on Modern Jewish Writing.* New York: Dutton, 1969, pp. 116–30. Reprinted as "Jewishness as Metaphor," in *Bernard Malamud and the Critics*, Leslie A. and Joyce W. Field, eds. New York: New York University Press, 1970, pp. 29–42.

Astro, Richard. "In the Heart of the Valley: Bernard Malamud's *A New Life.*" An original essay in *Bernard Malamud: A Collection of Critical Essays*, Leslie A. and Joyce W. Field, eds. Englewood Cliffs, N.J.: Prentice-Hall, 1975, pp. 143–155.

Baumbach, Jonathan. "The Economy of Love: The Novels of Bernard Malamud." *Kenyon Review* 25 (1963), 438–57.

Benson, Jackson J. "An Introduction: Bernard Malamud and the Haunting of America." *The Fiction of Bernard Malamud.* Richard Astro and Jackson J. Benson, eds. Corvallis: Oregon State University Press, 1977, pp. 13–43.

Bluefarb, Sam. "Bernard Malamud: The Scope of Caricature." *English Journal* 53 (1964), 319–26. Reprinted in *Bernard Malamud and the Critics*, Leslie A. and Joyce W. Field, eds. New York: New York University Press, 1970, pp. 137–50.

Dupee, Frederick Wilcox. "Malamud: The Uses and Abuses of Commitment." *"The King of the Cats," and other Remarks on Writers and Writing.* New York: Farrar, Straus & Giroux, 1965, pp. 156–63.

Field, Leslie A. "Portrait of the Artist as *Schlemiel.*" An original essay in *Bernard Malamud: A Collection of Critical Essays*, Leslie A. and Joyce W. Field, eds. Englewood Cliffs, N.J.: Prentice-Hall, 1975, pp. 117–29.

Friedman, Alan Warren. "Bernard Malamud: The Hero as Schnook." *Southern Review* NS 4 (1968), 927–44.

Reprinted as "The Hero as Schnook," in *Bernard Malamud and the Critics*, Leslie A. and Joyce W. Field, eds. New York: New York University Press, 1970, pp. 285–303.

Grebstein, Sheldon N. "Bernard Malamud and the Jewish Movement." *Contemporary American-Jewish Literature.* Irving Malin, ed. Bloomington: Indiana University Press, 1973, pp. 175–212. Reprinted in *Bernard Malamud: A Collection of Critical Essays*, Leslie A. and Joyce W. Field, eds. Englewood Cliffs, N.J.: Prentice-Hall, 1975, pp. 18–44.

Guttman, Allen. *The Jewish Writer in America: Assimilation and the Crisis of Identity.* New York: Oxford University Press, 1968, pp. 59–85.

Hassan, Ihab. "The Qualified Encounter: Three Novels by Buechner, Malamud, and Ellison." *Radical Innocence: Studies in the Contemporary American Novel.* Princeton: Princeton University Press, 1961, pp. 161–68. Reprinted as "The Qualified Encounter," in *Bernard Malamud and the Critics*, Leslie A. and Joyce W. Field, eds. New York: New York University Press, 1970, pp. 199–206.

Hicks, Granville. "Bernard Malamud." *Literary Horizons: A Quarter Century of American Fiction.* New York: New York University Press, 1970, pp. 65–83.

Hoyt, Charles A. "Bernard Malamud and the New Romanticism." *Contemporary American Novelists*, Harry Thornton Moore, ed. Carbondale: Southern Illinois University Press, 1964, pp. 65–79. Reprinted as "The New Romanticism," in *Bernard Malamud and the Critics*, Leslie A. and Joyce W. Field, eds. New York: New York University Press, 1970, pp. 171–84.

Kazin, Alfred. "The Magic and the Dread." *Contemporaries.* Boston: Little, Brown, 1962, pp. 202–7. Reprinted in *On Contemporary Literature*, Richard Kostelanetz, ed. New York: Avon, 1969, pp. 442–46.

Klein, Marcus. "Bernard Malamud: The Sadness of Goodness." *After Alienation.* Cleveland, Ohio: World Publishing Co., 1964, pp. 247–93. Reprinted as "The Sadness of Goodness," in *Bernard Malamud and the*

*Critics*, Leslie A. and Joyce W. Field, eds. New York: New York University Press, 1970, pp. 249–60.

Pinsker, Sanford. "The Schlemiel as Moral Bungler: Bernard Malamud's Ironic Heroes." *The Schlemiel as Metaphor: Studies in the Yiddish and American Jewish Novel*. Carbondale: Southern Illinois University Press, 1971, pp. 87–124. Reprinted as "Bernard Malamud's Ironic Heroes," in *Bernard Malamud: A Collection of Critical Essays*, Leslie A. and Joyce W. Field, eds. Englewood Cliffs, N.J.: Prentice-Hall, 1975, pp. 45–71.

Risty, Donald. "A Checklist of Malamud Criticism." *The Fiction of Bernard Malamud*. Richard Astro and Jackson J. Benson, eds. Corvallis: Oregon State University Press, 1977, pp. 163–90.

Roth, Philip. "Writing American Fiction. *Commentary* (March 1961), 223–33. Reprinted in *The American Novel Since World War II*, Marcus Klein, ed. Greenwich, Conn.: Fawcett Publications, 1969, pp. 142–58.

Rovit, Earl. "Bernard Malamud and the Jewish Literary Tradition." *Critique* (Winter–Spring 1960), 3–10. Reprinted as "The Jewish Literary Tradition," in *Bernard Malamud and the Critics*, Leslie A. and Joyce W. Field, eds. New York: New York University Press, 1970, pp. 3–10.

Schulz, Max F. "Bernard Malamud's Mythic Proletarians." *Radical Sophistication: Studies in Contemporary Jewish-American Novelists*. Athens: Ohio University Press, 1969, pp. 56–68. Reprinted as "Mythic Proletarians," in *Bernard Malamud and the Critics*, Leslie A. and Joyce W. Field, eds. New York: New York University Press, 1970, pp. 185–95.

Shear, Walter. "Culture Conflict in *The Assistant*." *Midwest Quarterly* (Summer 1966), 367–80. Reprinted as "Culture Conflict," in *Bernard Malamud and the Critics*, Leslie A. and Joyce W. Field, eds. New York: New York University Press, 1970, pp. 207–18.

Siegel, Ben. "Through a Glass Darkly: Bernard Malamud's Painful Views of the Self." *The Fiction of Bernard Malamud*. Richard Astro and Jackson J. Benson, eds.

Corvallis: Oregon State University Press, 1977, pp. 117–48.

Solotaroff, Theodore. "Bernard Malamud's Fiction: The Old Life and the New." *The Red Hot Vacuum and Other Pieces on the Writing of the Sixties.* New York: Atheneum, 1970, pp. 71–86. Originally appeared in *Commentary* (March 1962), 197–204. Reprinted as "The Old Life and the New," in *Bernard Malamud and the Critics*, Leslie A. and Joyce W. Field, eds. New York: New York University Press, 1970, pp. 235–48.

Wasserman, Earl R. "*The Natural*: Malamud's World Ceres." *Centennial Review* 9 (1965), 438–60. Reprinted in *Bernard Malamud and the Critics*, Leslie A. and Joyce W. Field, eds. New York: New York University Press, 1970, pp. 45–65.

Weinberg, Helen. *The New Novel in America: The Kafkan Mode in Contemporary Fiction.* Ithaca: Cornell University Press, 1970, pp. 165–85.

Wisse, Ruth R. "Requiem in Several Voices." *The Schlemiel as Modern Hero.* Chicago: University of Chicago Press, 1971, pp. 110–18.

# Index

# MODERN LITERATURE MONOGRAPHS

*In the same series (continued from page ii)*

CARSON MCCULLERS    *Richard M. Cook*
ALBERTO MORAVIA    *Jane E. Cottrell*
VLADIMIR NABOKOV    *Donald E. Morton*
ANAÏS NIN    *Bettina L. Knapp*
JOYCE CAROL OATES    *Ellen G. Friedman*
FLANNERY O'CONNOR    *Dorothy Tuck McFarland*
EUGENE O'NEILL    *Horst Frenz*
JOSÉ ORTEGA Y GASSET    *Franz Niedermayer*
GEORGE ORWELL    *Robert Kalechofsky*
KATHERINE ANNE PORTER    *John Edward Hardy*
EZRA POUND    *Jeannette Lander*
MARCEL PROUST    *James R. Hewitt*
RAINER MARIA RILKE    *Arnold Bauer*
J. N. SALINGER    *James Lundquist*
JEAN-PAUL SARTRE    *Liselotte Richter*
UPTON SINCLAIR    *Jon Yoder*
ISAAC BASHEVIS SINGER    *Irving Malin*
LINCOLN STEFFENS    *Robert Stinson*
JOHN STEINBECK    *Paul McCarthy*
JOHN UPDIKE    *Suzanne Henning Uphaus*
KURT VONNEGUT    *James Lundquist*
PETER WEISS    *Otto F. Best*
EDITH WHARTON    *Richard H. Lawson*
THORNTON WILDER    *Hermann Stresau*
THOMAS WOLFE    *Fritz Heinrich Ryssel*
VIRGINIA WOOLF    *Manly Johnson*
RICHARD WRIGHT    *David Bakish*
EMILE ZOLA    *Bettina L. Knapp*
CARL ZUCKMAYER    *Arnold Bauer*